80.1

Poems from the Hebrew

Poems from the

SELECTED BY

ETCHINGS BY

NEW YORK

HEBREW

ROBERT MEZEY

MOISHE SMITH

Thomas Y. Crowell Company

MANUFACTURED IN THE UNITED STATES OF AMERICA

ISBN 0–690–63685–7

1 2 3 4 5 6 7 8 9 10

Library of Congress Cataloging in Publication Data   Mezey, Robert, comp.
Poems from the Hebrew. (Poems of the world)   1. Hebrew poetry—
Translation into English. 2. English poetry—Translations from Hebrew.
I. Title.   PJ5059.E3M4 1973   892.4'1'008   75–132299
ISBN 0–690–63685–7

Acknowledgments

The compiler of *Poems from the Hebrew* and the Thomas Y. Crowell Company wish to thank the following authors, editors, publishers, and agents for granting permission to reprint copyrighted material. All possible care has been taken to trace ownership of every selection included and to make full acknowledgment for its use. If any errors have accidentally occurred, they will be corrected in subsequent editions, provided notification is sent to the publisher.

ACUM, LTD. of Tel-Aviv for Natan Alterman's "The Olive Tree" (trans. Robert Friend), "Moon" (trans. Ruth Finer Mintz), "Song to the Wife of His Youth," "Beyond Melody," and "The Silver Tray" (trans. Robert Mezey and Shula Starkman); for Yehuda Amichai's "On My Birthday" (trans. Ruth Finer Mintz), "Leaves Without Trees" (trans. Robert Mezey and Shula Starkman), "As for the World," "Mayor," "National Thoughts," "They Call Me," "To My Mother," "I Was the Moon," "In the Middle of This Century," and "The Place Where I Have Not Been" (trans. Assia Gutmann), copyright © 1968 by Yehuda Amichai; for David Avidan's "The Staircase" and for the selection from "Spanish Music in Winter" (trans. David Avidan) from *Megaovertone*; for Chaim Nachman Bialik's "Twilight Piece" (trans. Robert Friend), "O Thou Seer, Go, Flee Thee Away," "On Slaughter" (trans. Robert Mezey and Shula Starkman), and "Alone" (trans. A. C. Jacobs); for Yocheved Bat-Miriam's "Parting" (trans. Dom Moraes) and "Distance Spills Itself" (trans. Robert Mezey and Shula Starkman); for T. Carmi's "Snow in Jerusalem" and his lines from "Quatrains" (trans. Dom Moraes); for Yaakov Fichman's "Eve" (trans. Robert Friend); for Benjamin Galai's "Those Who Go, Not to Return" (trans. Robert Mezey and Shula Starkman); for Amir Gilboa's "Birth,"

"Blue and Red Poem" (trans. Robert Mezey and Shula Starkman), and "The Circle of Weeping" (trans. Ruth Finer Mintz); for Leah Goldberg's "Of Bloom" (trans. Dom Moraes) and "Song of the Strange Woman" (trans. Robert Friend); for Uri Zvi Greenberg's "The Hour," "With My God, the Smith," "Like a Woman," "The Great Sad One," "How It is," "There is a Box," "The Valley of Men," "On the Pole" (trans. Robert Mezey and Ben Zion Gold), "To the Mound of Corpses in the Snow" (trans. A. C. Jacobs), and "We Were Not Like Dogs" (trans. Robert Mezey); for Chaim Guri's "Odysseus" (trans. Robert Mezey and Shula Starkman), "Pictures of the Jews," and "Piyyut for Rosh Hashana" (trans. Ruth Finer Mintz); for Omer Hillel's "At the Scorpion's Ascent" (trans. Sholom J. Kahn) from *Israel Argosy;* for Yehiel Mar's "Handfuls of Wind" (trans. Ruth Finer Mintz); for Rachel's "Revolt," "My Dead" (trans. Robert Mezey), and "His Wife" (trans. Robert Friend); for David Rokeah's "Blind Angel" (trans. Robert Mezey and Shula Starkman); for Natan Sach's "I Saw" (trans. Robert Mezey); for Shin Shalom's "Incense" (trans. Robert Friend) and "Not So Simple" (trans. Robert Mezey); for the lines from Avraham Shlonsky's "Jezrael" (trans. Ruth Finer Mintz) and "Sabbath Stars" (trans. Dom Moraes); for Zalman Shneour's "Stop Playing" (trans. Robert Mezey); for Saul Tchernichovsky's "Man Is Nothing But," "The Grave," and "Your People Are Drowning in Blood" (trans. Robert Mezey and Shula Starkman).

A. S. BARNES COMPANY, INC., for Meyer Waxman's translation of Abraham ibn Ezra's "Born Without a Star" from *A History of Jewish Literature* by Meyer Waxman.

CURTIS BROWN, LTD. and ANDRÉ DEUTSCH for the selection from T. Carmi's *The Brass Serpent* (trans. Dom Moraes).

PETER EVERWINE and SHULA STARKMAN for the translation of T. Carmi's "The Condition" from *TransPacific.*

DAVID GOLDSTEIN for his translations of Samuel the Prince's "War," Solomon ibn Gabirol's "An Apple for Isaac" and "In the Morning I Look for You," and Judah Halevi's "To Moses ibn Ezra in Christian Spain" and Abraham ibn Ezra's "You are a servant of the living God, Why have you enslaved yourself to the earth?" from *Hebrew Poems from Spain*, edited and translated by David Goldstein, copyright © 1965 by David Goldstein, published by Schocken Books Inc.

HARPER & ROW PUBLISHERS, INC., for the translations by Assia Gutmann of Yehuda Amichai's "As for the World," "National Thoughts," "Mayor," "They Call Me," "To My Mother," "I Was the Moon," "In the Middle of This Century," and "The Place Where I Have Not Been" from *Poems: Yehuda Amichai*, copyright © 1968 by Yehuda Amichai. English translation copyright © 1968, 1969 by Assia Gutmann.

OHIO UNIVERSITY PRESS for the translation by Dom Moraes of the lines from *The Brass Serpent*, copyright © 1964 by Ohio University Press.

DAVID ROKEAH for his poems "Blind Angel" (trans. Robert Mezey and Shula Starkman) and "The Wall" (trans. Bernard Lewis).

SCHOCKEN BOOKS INC., for "The Shepherd's Song" from *Tales of the Hasidim: The Early Masters*, by Martin Buber (trans. Olga Marx), copyright © 1947 by Schocken Books Inc.; and for the translations of David Goldstein of Abraham ibn Ezra's "You are a servant of the living God, Why have you enslaved yourself to the earth?" from *Hebrew Poems from Spain*, Samuel the Prince's "War," Solomon ibn Gabirol's "An Apple for Isaac" and "In the Morning I Look for You," and Judah Halevi's "To Moses ibn Ezra in Christian Spain" from *Hebrew Poems from Spain*, edited and translated by David Goldstein, copyright © 1965 by David Goldstein, published by Schocken Books Inc.

UNIVERSITY OF CALIFORNIA PRESS and RUTH FINER MINTZ for the translations by Ruth Finer Mintz of Avraham Shlonsky's selection from "Jezrael," Natan Alterman's "Moon," Chaim Guri's "Pictures of the Jews" and "Piyyut for Rosh Hashana," and Yehuda Amichai's "On My Birthday" from *Modern Hebrew Poetry* edited and translated by Ruth Finer Mintz, 1966. Originally published by the University of California Press; reprinted by permission of The Regents of the University of California.

POEMS OF THE WORLD
Under the editorship of Lillian Morrison

POEMS FROM AFRICA
Selected by Samuel Allen

POEMS FROM FRANCE
Selected by William Jay Smith

POEMS FROM THE GERMAN
Selected by Helen Plotz

POEMS FROM THE HEBREW
Selected by Robert Mezey

POEMS FROM INDIA
Selected by Daisy Aldan

POEMS FROM IRELAND
Selected by William Cole

POEMS FROM ITALY
Selected by William Jay Smith

This book is for Ronald

Who is great here, who is small
In the kingdom of work and very flesh?

Contents

Introduction   I

The Ancient Poems   15

The Poets of Moorish Spain   55

The Modern Poets   69

INDEX OF TITLES   151

INDEX OF FIRST LINES   154

INDEX OF POETS   158

INDEX OF TRANSLATORS   159

Rabbi Zusya once passed a meadow where a swine-herd in the midst of his flock was playing a song on a willow-flute. He came close and listened until he had learned it and could take it away with him. In this way the song of David, the shepherd-boy, was freed from its long captivity.

—TALES OF THE HASIDIM

1   Introduction

MORE than four thousand years ago, a band of nomads roamed the semiarid lands between the Negev Desert and the Sinai Peninsula. Very little is known about these people. Perhaps they were the Apiru—the name appears in ancient papyri, and *Hebrew* is a plausible corruption. There was little to distinguish them among the many tribes who tended flocks or vines in that country; their language was like other languages spoken there, their gods like the other gods.

Their chief god was Yahweh, deity of a sacred volcano—"pillar of cloud by day, pillar of fire by night." Over the two or three hundred years they were invading, conquering, and settling the land of Canaan, they began to think of themselves as special, party to a covenant with this Yahweh. It must have been, in the beginning, a simple deal: he would throw his weight on the side of their armies; they would establish his supremacy over the lesser deities of the place. They could hardly have guessed where this agreement was to lead them.

In the year 1000 B.C. or thereabouts, they became a kingdom, but were soon divided by class struggle and civil war: Israel, the northern half, was swallowed up by Assyria in 721 B.C. and its people deported, never to be heard of again. Judah in the south managed to survive a while longer, but it was overwhelmed by one empire after another—Babylon, Persia, Macedon, Rome—and by the sixth century B.C. the political annihilation of the Hebrews was largely accomplished.

One might expect that at this point, shorn of all sovereignty, they would vanish into stronger peoples, as did their northern brothers and so many Canaanite tribes. But they endured. During their brief national existence, they had created a religion and a culture that would compel them and sustain them as a people for more than two thousand years; in country after country, despised and envied, raped and murdered, locked into ghettos or driven out to wander the face of the earth, somehow they endured.

If Rome was the father of what we presume to call Western civilization, the Jews were its mother, for out of them, as out of a womb, came Christianity. An unwilling gift, that cross, and soon turned into the old sword of conquest, but they gave other gifts, very beautiful. One is the seed of this alphabet in which I am now writing; another is the great literature which has survived the teeth of three millennia and is still flourishing today.

It is a literature at once familiar and strange. At its heart lie preconceptions about the nature of reality and about human destiny which have been the assumptions of our religions and sciences throughout Western history, and it is charged with a complex moral consciousness which we must recognize, like it or not, as our own. Yet its language is very foreign to our eyes and ears, its sense of time fluid and ambiguous, and its perception of structure and relationship hard to convey in a European tongue.

True, the Bible is one of the central books of our civilization; the King James Version may well be the supreme classic of the English language. But it has ceased to be common knowledge. It is one of those books which everyone loves and few read. Many people who think they revere it would be greatly offended to learn what it has to say about how they earn their livings and treat their neighbors.

Which brings us to the unpleasant problem of morality. It is hard to speak of Hebrew literature without considering its almost constant preoccupation with morality, but I do not wish to introduce these poems or express my love for them on the basis of their moral attitudes. The Bible is, among other things, a record of the development of religious and moral consciousness among a particular people over a period of a thousand years. Much of the ancient law is as harsh and loveless as the Code of Hammurabi. Many of the poems are gloating celebrations of cunning and brute force or savage calls for vengeance. Kenneth Rexroth has called the Old Testament "one of the most disagreeable books in all the unpleasant history of religion. . . . The early Gnostics were perfectly right," he says. "What the Old Testament teaches is not virtue but 'sin,' murder, adultery, deception, anger, jealousy, above all, *disloyalty*. . . . No other sacred book is so utterly immoral." This judgment has little to do, I think, with the great school of mystical and prophetic thought that culminates in the life of Jesus, but it is certainly true of the Pentateuch with its endless treachery and cruelty and its vindictive and deceitful God, of the histories, and to some extent, of the Writings. Even in the great body of modern Hebrew poetry, one can find the ugly scars of too many old wounds, proof of the dictum that those to whom evil is done do evil in return—or would like to.

But poetry is more than morality, and in a profound sense, beyond it, indifferent to it. Poetry is always struggling to enter the Kingdom of Heaven, which is simply utmost expansion of consciousness, and there, morality does not exist. A drop of rain is neither moral nor immoral; it *is,* and a poet celebrates its reality with his own—an act of vision and not of judgment. Morality is for slaves and exiles, all of us who have not entered the Kingdom, including poets. Poetry is freedom. As it is said, "Death and life are in the power of the tongue: and they that love it shall eat the fruit thereof."

Poetry, being made out of words by men, must reckon with the horrors and sufferings of this world, and it creates values which, like men, are very far from perfect. But at times divine truth enters a man as breath enters his lungs; he may be a drunk, a syphilitic, a thief, but such a man, we say, is *inspired,* and like the voice from the whirlwind, he sings a reality that dwarfs and shames our petty quarreling over good and evil. This reality is the bread of the spirit, without which we live in wretched poverty.

THE ANCIENT POEMS

Many of these songs and passages have been ascribed traditionally to this or that shining name, but they are, in fact, anonymous. It is most unlikely that any of the psalms attributed to David were actually composed by him, for they were written many centuries after his death; some scholars say that if we have any writing by his hand, it is possibly the elegy for Saul and Jonathan with which this anthology begins. Even in the prophetical books, it is usually impossible to know how faithfully the visions were recorded. The books were put together after the deaths of the seers whose names they bear, and it is easy to show that most of them contain a great deal of extraneous material. Take Isaiah, which purports to be the sayings of one man—it is made up of the utterances of

[3

at least three different poets, along with various interpolations, oracles, biographical notes, one long passage more or less lifted from II Kings, and probably tags and fragments from a dozen earlier works no longer extant.

Such difficulties are general throughout the Bible. Almost none of the ancient literature has been preserved in its original form. Every book passed through many hands and was edited and re-edited, sometimes centuries later, and often with the motive of making the ideas of the original work conform to what some priest thought they should be. They were tampered with so extensively that hundreds of passages are utterly confused, self-contradictory, and incomprehensible.

We should remember also that there must have been a great many poems and tales that are lost to us because they were not admitted into Scripture. What we have, with one or two exceptions, is sacred literature; the exceptions suggest how much great work was allowed to slip into oblivion. The Song of Songs, whatever else it may be, has little to do with religion; it has stolen a ride into immortality because the Rabbis and later the Christians mistakenly believed it to be the work of Solomon and therefore felt obliged to torture its clear eroticism into one pompous allegory or another.* One wonders how many beautiful poems of love and friendship, how many drinking songs, epigrams, and festival chants, have perished because no one thought to attribute them to Solomon or Moses or God himself.

Much of what we have—folktales, devotional poems, mythology, wisdom—bears a close resemblance to other ancient writings. One finds parallels constantly in the surviving Egyptian texts, in the Sumerian, Akkadian, and Babylonian. But certain ideas were peculiar to the Hebrews—for instance, the whole mystique of the covenant, and that strange phenomenon we call prophecy.

The four hundred years during which the prophets erupted were a

---

* The interested reader should look up Leroy Waterman's book, *The Song of Songs Interpreted as a Dramatic Poem*, which tries to make some sense out of the badly garbled text. Waterman sees The Song of Songs as a love poem with political overtones. He argues that it was composed in the northern kingdom shortly after the civil war (thus the unflattering picture of Solomon) and celebrates the story of the peasant girl Abishag, her fidelity to her northern shepherd boy, and her brave refusal to enter Solomon's harem. Also worth reading is John Logan's beautiful and very personal version in *Ghosts of the Heart*.

mysterious and powerful age. An immense spiritual energy was manifesting, incarnating itself, all over the planet. During this time Buddha, Zoroaster, Plato, and Confucius lived and taught—not to mention Lao-tzu and maybe Patanjali—and in one tiny country arose Amos, Isaiah, Micah, Jeremiah, Ezekiel, Hosea, and a host of lesser visionaries and messengers.

Think of it. It is early morning, let us say, before dawn, sometime in the eighth century before Christ. The royal tabernacle of the northern king, Jeroboam II. A man stands up and begins to shout, interrupting the services, denouncing the priest and the congregation. He accuses them of swindling and bullying the poor. He says their empty piety is disgusting to God. He predicts disaster—invasion, captivity, a bad end for everybody. The priest is beside himself with anger and fear; you can imagine the response of the congregation. This man, this Amos, is a loner, a rough peasant, an interloper from Judah—what the rich and powerful of every age like to call "an outside agitator." That morning they would have called him a communist if they had known how.

The Hebrew word for prophet is *nabi,* which probably means "one who bubbles over." It was not a pleasant word; people sneered, as when they asked, "Is Saul also among the prophets?" This should not surprise anyone. People have never enjoyed hearing some long-haired, disreputable character tell them that their whole life is a lie, their laws a crime, their religion hypocrisy and fraud. Yet it is usually true. What does Micah say? "Wherewith shall I come before the Lord, and bow myself before the high God? shall I come before him with burnt offerings, with calves of a year old? Will the Lord be pleased with thousands of rams, or with ten thousands of rivers of oil? shall I give my firstborn for my transgression, the fruit of my body for the sin of my soul? He hath shewed thee, O man, what is good; and what doth the Lord require of thee, but to do justly, and to love mercy, and to walk humbly with thy God?"

The greatness of these wandering mystics, bubbling over with visions, with mad sacred poetry, was to understand that justice is more important than ritual, to insist that religion and ethics are inseparable. Of course, they foretold the future, and rather accurately, but there was nothing necessarily supernatural in that. Couldn't any poet, any careful observer, have told the Israelites their days were numbered?

Hear the voice of the bard, telling the Americans much the same. The prophetic voice, now ecstatic, now accusing, is still alive in our own time, the voice of Bob Dylan and Malcolm X, of Allen Ginsberg and Lenny Bruce. Isn't it the same temper that drives the revolutionary priests of Europe and Latin America, that sends the best of our youth into the streets to rave against the shamelessness of their country? Isn't it the rage, the grief, the hidden plea of prophecy we hear as they curse the godless state and demand paradise now? Read Hosea; then read Ginsberg's "Death to Van Gogh's Ear."

INTERLUDE IN MOORISH SPAIN

For a long time after the close of the biblical period, the poetic genius of the Jews seemed to have dried up. Prayer and liturgy continued to be written, but it was greatly inferior to what had gone before. All the fervor, subtlety, and wit of the best minds went into the making of commentaries, homiletics, legends, and mystic systems, into Talmud, Midrash, Cabbala—strange, rich, wonderful books through which the community of exiled and scattered Jews stayed alive. But it was not until the ninth or tenth century in Spain that Hebrew poetry began to flower once again.

At the end of the seventh century, the Jews of Spain were suffering as usual, like Jews everywhere. This time it was the Visigoths, and the story was the same: homes confiscated, synagogues burned, children sold for slaves, many people killed. But deliverance was at hand. In 711, the Saracens invaded the Iberian Peninsula and, seeking allies against the Christian armies, armed the ghettos. When Christian power was ended in a large part of the country, the Jews, who had helped to end it, began to breathe again. The Arabs granted them citizenship, and in the course of time, they helped their liberators to build a high and dazzling civilization.

Life was not always easy; fighting flamed up in this town or that; a few of the Moorish kings were fanatics; but for the most part, Jew and Muslim lived in amity. There were prosperous Jewish communities everywhere: in Granada, Sevilla, Córdoba. Jews became mathematicians, bankers, surgeons, even generals and ministers of state. Schools were opened, and philosophy and esoteric learning flourished. Artists found patrons, and painting and architecture were revived. In response to the challenges of new sects, the Scriptures were studied with new intensity, and many fruitful discoveries were made. And the poets, eager to throw off the artificialities of earlier verse and stimulated by the brilliance of Arabic poetry, created a body of work of great splendor and enduring importance.

Religious themes were predominant, so many of the poets being also Talmudists and Cabbalists. But once again, secular poetry was written. Borrowing liberally from the Arabs, they developed an intricate quantitative meter and began to use rhyme—striving to regain the vigor and simplicity of biblical poetry, they began by abandoning its characteristic sonority, the rough two-beat or three-beat unrhymed couplet. They were excited by new images and conventions, and in the meantime could hardly ignore what the Arabic poets were talking about. So they wrote songs of love and friendship, poems about wine, satires and witty complaints, and though their best gift was for sacred poetry, much of the worldly verse is very fine, and it unquestionably extended the range of the art for their successors.

Most translations of the medieval poetry are horrible. My selection might have been much larger, but reading the versions of Emma Lazarus and other well-meaning persons, no one would believe that Gabirol and Halevi were great poets or that anyone had ever thought so. Having so few poems that I was willing to use, I was tempted to drop this section entirely, but even this handful of poems gives some idea, I think, of the humanity and richness of feeling in the poetry of Moorish Spain and indicates a beautiful continuity from the shepherds and warriors of twenty-five centuries ago to the writers living today in the beleaguered cities of Israel.

But more than this, it is good to remember, in a time when Jews and Arabs are preparing to murder one another by the thousands, that it has not always been so. Once they were friends and co-creators, as they should be, for they are brothers, they come from the same blood and the same part of the world, and their languages, music, and life styles have been very close.

In one of these poems, Judah Halevi, sick with longing to see Jerusalem, speaks of himself as lying in the chains of the Arab. This is a pretty figure and fits his mood, but we should not take it too literally. It is true that at the time it was written, unrelenting warfare between Muslim and Christian had begun to uproot and devastate the Jews; the life they had made in Spain was falling apart. But if Halevi could have looked into the future and seen how Jews were to fare in Christian Europe, and how they will fare as an armed aggressive state in the heart of Islam, maybe he would have kissed those easy chains.

THE MODERN POETS

To a certain extent, modern Hebrew poetry is more accessible to us than the ancient or medieval literature. The modern poets inhabit our world and endure with us its emptiness, its violence, its apparently insoluble problems. They live, as we do, on the edge of the abyss. Still, their poetry is very different from ours. Wearier? Older? More bloodstained? The reader must make of it what he can. To understand how it came to be what it is, it is necessary to grasp a complex history which is beyond the scope of this essay.

One would have to study the seventeenth and eighteenth centuries when Jews were slowly beginning to emerge from the ghetto; the collapse of the great messianic movements, and the despair that followed the first wild hope; the hardship and insecurity of Jewish life in the Pales of Settlement; and the rich peasant culture of the *shtetl.* One would have to understand the ideology of the Enlightenment, which began with the insistence that Jews become truly European and bourgeois and give up their orthodoxies for the rationalist and scientific ideals of the new age, and ended, as Jews were disburdened of their naive dreams of integration, in fanatical nationalism. One would have to read Herzl and others whose early formulations of Zionism inflamed the minds of Jews everywhere. And one would have to learn something about Hasidism.

How can I explain Hasidism in a few sentences? Well, it was a religious revival movement which began in eighteenth-century Poland in response to the deterioration of rabbinical authority and the growing alienation of the Jews from the old sources of spiritual energy. Founded by Israel Baal-Shem-Tov, who was a great saint like Jesus or Ramakrishna, it put aside traditional asceticism, affirming physical life and the desires of the body and proclaiming a condition of joy. Every moment, every detail of daily life, was to be sanctified and transformed by love for God and for his creation. The duty of man was not to avoid what was gross and profane, but to redeem it. The sexual act, song and dance, the sharing of food and wine—these were mystical sacraments by means of which one might transcend personality and stand outside one's self, in ecstasy. The Hasidim, stoned on their own music and fervor, would dance and sing for hours, pressing the holy scrolls to their breasts. Dogma was nothing. The great thing was to accept suffering with joy, and to cherish the natural world and the blessings of conscious work. And as Jews had done for two thousand years, the Hasidim longed for Zion.

The reader who wishes to learn more about this profoundly beautiful sect will find no better introduction than Martin Buber's *Tales of the Hasidim*. I have described it briefly here because it had a greater and healthier influence on the modern poets than any other aspect of Jewish religious life. A very large number of them came from Hasidic homes, and though many abandoned orthodox Judaism, the Hasidic sense of community and redemption through work and love, as well as its wide anecdotal wisdom, remained a warm part of their thought and feeling.

It is impossible to say when modern Hebrew poetry began, it began at so many different times in so many different countries, but almost everyone agrees that its first great accomplishments were the work of the Russians Bialik and Tchernichovsky, who are to Hebrew poetry what Williams and Pound are to American. A great deal of poetry had been written during the four centuries since the Jews' expulsion from Spain, but most of it is not memorable. It had been thousands of years since Hebrew was a vernacular, and it was perhaps inevitable that its poetry would decay into bookish ornament and didacticism. The genius of Bialik and Tchernichovsky was to begin to free the language of the tiresome rhetoric of the past and to create an idiom more suitable to the mouths of nineteenth-century men.

Medieval Hebrew had been a literary language to begin with, and its stiffness, together with the multiplicity of dialects and styles, led to its rapid deterioration as a medium for poetry. It may be that the chief value of Enlightenment propaganda and of Zionism was that they made a cult of Hebrew and gave great impetus to the creation of a modern language. Mishnaic and medieval Hebrew were bypassed, and the classical Hebrew of the Bible became the model for the new tongue. This was a happy decision, for it restored to Hebrew a purity and simplicity that it had lacked for a very long time.

It is a difficult and exciting language for poetry, this Hebrew simultaneously classical and modern. More than one writer has observed that the idiom and imagery of the Bible are immediately familiar to Israelis, and while one continual problem for the poet is to avoid biblical association when he does not want it, the splendor of ancient myth and song is always there for him and gives his work a marvelous resonance and subtlety. And it gives him a vocabulary in which he can speak simply and naturally of the cosmic and the eternal, whereas in our language many such words have grown hollow and pretentious and hard to use.

For the twentieth-century poets, the old obsession with Zion and the endless lamentation over the fate of the Jews were sharpened by two overwhelming realities. One was the fierce and successful struggle to establish a new homeland in Palestine. Jews had been drifting to Palestine, writers among them, for a long time, but it was during the large waves of immigration after the Russian Revolution and the two World Wars that many poets, seeing that their lives in Europe were finished, threw in their lot with the pioneers. For great numbers of these people, Zionism and socialism had taken the place of the old faith, and it was this intense political ardor that helped to sustain them through the long years of poverty and backbreaking toil on the land. They set up *kibbutzim*—collective farms, little self-contained societies, some religious, some devoutly Marxist—and they armed themselves, for like the Moabites and Amorites of antiquity, the Arab peasantry did not take kindly to the intrusion. After all, they had lived there for so many centuries; it was their home. But these Jews felt that this was their last chance for survival in a world which had made it clear that their survival was of no interest whatsoever. Their manifesto during those years was Lamdam's long poem *Masada*; Masada was the name of the mountain fortress in which the Judeans fought their last desperate battle against the Romans. Palestine was the last ditch. The poets joined in the struggle for life, and many worked on the land and celebrated the commune and the grinding physical labor with almost religious passion. How badly they wanted something to believe in. Yet they were nagged by doubt, and side by side with poems of wild exuberance and faith, one finds troubled poems, poems touched by boredom and fear and despair.

The other impossible reality was genocide. A young American, for whom the Nazis' Final Solution is something remembered from a history book, can hardly imagine the terror of those years. Then, too, torture and mass murder have become so commonplace in our world that we can watch it on television and then sit down to our big dinners; since our own nation is busy committing similar crimes, we cannot afford to imagine them too vividly. But it was the Third Reich, with the tacit approval or at least the indifference of the whole civilized world, that first showed us how efficient murder could be. In 1944, it was not so easy to kill six million people. It has become much easier.

The ultimate horror was that the beast was not only German. It seemed that the whole world was conspiring to rid itself of Jews once and for all. "Paying Germany back in her own coin, everything under the skullcap of the heavens that called itself a democracy condemned her, in reprisal for her anti-Semitism, to keep her Jews. The punishment was brilliant. It was applied at the precise moment when Nazism, out of patience, suffocating with Yiddishness, opened Hamburg to Jewish emigration. Draining toward that port by the tens of thousands, the German Jews were brought up painfully against democracy's order of the day—'No visa.' A few handfuls set sail anyway. In the name of humanity, they were not sunk, but were permitted to die at anchor in London, Marseilles, New York, Tel Aviv . . . and at any anchor they wished." That is from André Schwarz-Bart's *The Last of the Just*, a very great novel and one of the few books that will give you some idea of what it was like to be a Jew. To be a Jew was impossible.

Thinking of all this, it is hard to blame the Israelis for their fear and their weapons. For two thousand years Jews did not bear arms, and their reward was to be taunted and killed. It is easy to tell them now that they will not survive with rockets and napalm, that they must approach their enemies in a spirit of love and reconciliation, but who has the right to tell them such things? We Americans especially have no right.

The new generation of poets, most of whom were born in Israel or came there in childhood and lived through the partition and the first bitter war with the Arabs, does not seem to lean as their elders did on the militant ideology that had been a kind of religion for the pioneers and the resistance fighters. This is not to say that they are not Zionists and socialists; some of them are, and probably almost all are nationalists. But nationhood is a fact for these young artists, and they have seen that it does not solve the problems of life. The anxiety and despair that descended on so many postwar literatures, the bleak recognition that perhaps the problems have no solutions, has manifested itself in Israeli poetry, which has grown more and more personal and subjective and less specifically "Jewish."

The great predecessors, Alterman and Shlonsky especially, continue to have an influence, but contemporary work in America and Europe is read and taken seriously. Though some of the older writers, like Greenberg, have attacked this cosmopolitanism, it is surely a healthy thing. Hebrew poetry is less parochial now; there is an ease and naturalness in it that was lacking even in the great work of the thirties and forties.

Israeli poets are so numerous and so various, it is foolhardy to generalize about them. Introductions encourage easy generalizations, and this one is no exception, but I have the feeling that a poetry of great vision and authority, an art to rival or surpass the art of Alterman or Greenberg, is beginning to flower in modern Israel. Some of the young poets have already given signs of mastery, and it is astonishing to realize how many gifted and prolific writers have emerged in this tiny country of three million people. Many of them are not represented in this book: there was not enough space; there were not enough impressive or even decent translations. But I hope that the twenty-five or thirty poems printed here will show something of the honesty and delicacy of the new poetry, its power, its originality, its promise for the future of the art and of the nation.

A FEW EXPLANATIONS

The quality of available translations had a great deal to do with the final shape of this book. Every translator, every editor of translations, is condemned to make a ceremonial declaration that his task is impossible. Let me say only that except for the King James Version of the Scriptures, Hebrew poetry has not been particularly blessed with luminous translations.

I tried to use work by every poet of importance, but certainly there are many good poets who are absent simply because there are no adequate English versions of their poems, or if there are, I could not find them. Shimoni, Halkin, Hameiri—these are a few of the names that spring to mind of poets I would like to have included. Yonatan Ratosh is another—a wonderful and unusual poet who wanted his people to forget the West and turn back to their ancient origins, concealed by priests and lost in exile.

The size of each selection was dictated by the same considerations. I would otherwise have given many more pages to father Bialik and to Tchernichovsky, in my opinion the greatest of the early moderns. Similarly, the fact that Judah Halevi is represented by six poems and Moses ibn Ezra by one does not signify their relative merit.

I decided not to supply notes because I wanted this little anthology to be a vivid experience for readers for whom this literature is fairly unfamiliar, and notes, I felt, would give it the cumbersome feel of a textbook. For the most part, I chose poems that do not require any special lore. The medieval and modern poems contain many echoes of biblical lines, but recognition is not essential to one's simple pleasure, and anyway most of the paraphrases and allusions will ring for the reader who has even a rough acquaintance with the King James Bible. Moreover, some of these references are clarified by other poems in the book. For example, when Halevi in his little poem to Moses ibn Ezra asks why he has settled in Christian Spain, "Why does the dew of Hermon settle on Gilboa," the reader who remembers the first poem in this book, the elegy for Saul and Jonathan, will get the idea, even if he does not happen to recall Psalm 133.

Finally, I must acknowledge several large debts. To Ben Zion Gold, who introduced me to the poetry of Uri Zvi Greenberg and spent many long and beautiful hours with me, translating and talking and worrying. To Shula Starkman, whose help was invaluable in getting other modern poems into English. To Bill Merwin for turning me on to Amichai's poem, "The Place Where I Have Not Been." To three books that were very helpful: *Modern Hebrew Poetry* by Ruth Finer Mintz; *Hebrew Poems from Spain* by David Goldstein; and *The Modern Hebrew Poem Itself*, edited by Stanley Burnshaw, T. Carmi, and Ezra Spicehandler; and to Robert Alter's essay "Poetry in Israel." To Philip Starkman and Sandra Flanery for kindly helping me to get some books I needed. And to Ollie who, understanding that in a labor of love, the love comes easier to me than the labor, kept after me and loved me and saw it through.

ROBERT MEZEY

Cañellas, Spain

The

ANCIENT POEMS

Ye shall have a song, as in the
night when a holy solemnity is
kept; and gladness of heart, as
when one goeth with a pipe to
come into the mountain of
the Lord . . .

—ISAIAH 30:29

DAVID'S LAMENTATION

The beauty of Israel is slain upon thy high places: how are the mighty fallen!

Tell it not in Gath, publish it not in the streets of Askelon; lest the daughters of the Philistines rejoice, lest the daughters of the uncircumcised triumph.

Ye mountains of Gilboa, let there be no dew, neither let there be rain upon you, nor fields of offerings: for there the shield of the mighty is vilely cast away, the shield of Saul, as though he had not been anointed with oil.

From the blood of the slain, from the fat of the mighty, the bow of Jonathan turned not back, and the sword of Saul returned not empty.

Saul and Jonathan were lovely and pleasant in their lives, and in their death they were not divided: they were swifter than eagles, they were stronger than lions.

Ye daughters of Israel, weep over Saul, who clothed you in scarlet, with other delights, who put on ornaments of gold upon your apparel.

How are the mighty fallen in the midst of the battle! O Jonathan, thou wast slain in thine high places.

I am distressed for thee, my brother Jonathan: very pleasant hast thou been unto me: thy love to me was wonderful, passing the love of women.

How are the mighty fallen, and the weapons of war perished!

II SAMUEL 1:19–27

THE COMPLAINT TO GOD

Is there not an appointed time to man upon earth? are not his days also like the days of an hireling?
As a servant earnestly desireth the shadow, and as an hireling looketh for the reward of his work:
So am I made to possess months of vanity, and wearisome nights are appointed to me.

When I lie down, I say, When shall I arise, and the night be gone? and I am full of tossings to and fro unto the dawning of the day.

My flesh is clothed with worms and clods of dust; my skin is broken, and become loathsome.
My days are swifter than a weaver's shuttle, and are spent without hope.

O remember that my life is wind: mine eye shall no more see good.
The eye of him that hath seen me shall see me no more: thine eyes are upon me, and I am not.

As the cloud is consumed and vanisheth away: so he that goeth down to the grave shall come up no more.

He shall return no more to his house, neither shall his place know him any more.

Therefore I will not refrain my mouth; I will speak in the anguish of my spirit; I will complain in the bitterness of my soul.

Am I a sea, or a whale, that thou settest a watch over me?

When I say, My bed shall comfort me, my couch shall ease my complaint;

Then thou scarest me with dreams, and terrifiest me through visions:

So that my soul chooseth strangling, and death rather than my life.

I loathe it; I would not live alway: let me alone; for my days are vanity.

What is man, that thou shouldest magnify him? and that thou shouldest set thine heart upon him?

And that thou shouldest visit him every morning, and try him every moment?

How long wilt thou not depart from me, nor let me alone till I swallow down my spittle?

I have sinned; what shall I do unto thee, O thou preserver of men? why hast thou set me as a mark against thee, so that I am a burden to myself?

And why dost thou not pardon my transgression, and take away mine iniquity? for now shall I sleep in the dust; and thou shalt seek me in the morning, but I shall not be.

JOB 7

I WILL EXTOL THEE, O LORD

I will extol thee, O Lord; for thou hast lifted me up, and hast not made my foes to rejoice over me.

O Lord my God, I cried unto thee, and thou hast healed me.

O Lord, thou hast brought up my soul from the grave: thou hast kept me alive, that I should not go down to the pit.

Sing unto the Lord, O ye saints of his, and give thanks at the remembrance of his holiness.

For his anger endureth but a moment; in his favour is life: weeping may endure for a night, but joy cometh in the morning.

And in my prosperity I said, I shall never be moved.

Lord, by thy favour thou hast made my mountain to stand strong: thou didst hide thy face, and I was troubled.

I cried to thee, O Lord; and unto the Lord I made supplication.

What profit is there in my blood, when I go down to the pit? Shall the dust praise thee? shall it declare thy truth?

Hear, O Lord, and have mercy upon me: Lord, be thou my helper.

Thou hast turned for me my mourning into dancing: thou hast put off my sackcloth, and girded me with gladness;

To the end that my glory may sing praise to thee, and not be silent. O Lord my God, I will give thanks unto thee for ever.

PSALM 30

A PRAYER TO BE RESTORED
TO THE SANCTUARY

How amiable are thy tabernacles, O Lord of hosts!

My soul longeth, yea, even fainteth for the courts of the Lord: my heart and my flesh crieth out for the living God.

Yea, the sparrow hath found a house, and the swallow a nest for herself, where she may lay her young, even thine altars, O Lord of hosts, my King, and my God.

Blessed are they that dwell in thy house: they will be still praising thee. Selah.

Blessed is the man whose strength is in thee; in whose heart are the ways of them.

Who passing through the valley of Baca make it a well; the rain also filleth the pools.

They go from strength to strength, every one of them in Zion appeareth before God.

O Lord God of hosts, hear my prayer: give ear, O God of Jacob.

Behold, O God our shield, and look upon the face of thine anointed.

For a day in thy courts is better than a thousand. I had rather be a doorkeeper in the house of my God, than to dwell in the tents of wickedness.

For the Lord God is a sun and shield: the Lord will give grace and glory: no good thing will he withhold from them that walk uprightly.

O Lord of hosts, blessed is the man that trusteth in thee.

PSALM 84

LORD, THOU HAST BEEN OUR DWELLING PLACE

Lord, thou hast been our dwelling place in all generations.

Before the mountains were brought forth, or ever thou hadst formed the earth and the world, even from everlasting to everlasting, thou art God.

Thou turnest man to destruction; and sayest, Return, ye children of men.

For a thousand years in thy sight are but as yesterday when it is past, and as a watch in the night

Thou carriest them away as with a flood; they are as a sleep: in the morning they are like grass which groweth up.

In the morning it flourisheth, and groweth up; in the evening it is cut down, and withereth.

For we are consumed by thine anger, and by thy wrath are we troubled.

[23

Thou hast set our iniquities before thee, our secret sins in the light of thy countenance.

For all our days are passed away in thy wrath: we spend our years as a tale that is told.

The days of our years are threescore years and ten; and if by reason of strength they be fourscore years, yet is their strength labour and sorrow; for it is soon cut off, and we fly away.

Who knoweth the power of thine anger? even according to thy fear, so is thy wrath.

So teach us to number our days, that we may apply our hearts unto wisdom.

Return, O Lord, how long? and let it repent thee concerning thy servants.

O satisfy us early with thy mercy; that we may rejoice and be glad all our days.

Make us glad according to the days wherein thou hast afflicted us, and the years wherein we have seen evil.

Let thy work appear unto thy servants, and thy glory unto their children.

And let the beauty of the Lord our God be upon us: and establish thou the work of our hands upon us; yea, the work of our hands establish thou it.

PSALM 90

A MEDITATION ON PROVIDENCE

Bless the Lord, O my soul. O Lord my God, thou art very great; thou art clothed with honour and majesty.

Who coverest thyself with light as with a garment: who stretchest out the heavens like a curtain:

Who layeth the beams of his chambers in the waters: who maketh the clouds his chariot: who walketh upon the wings of the wind:

Who maketh his angels spirits; his ministers a flaming fire:

Who laid the foundations of the earth, that it should not be removed for ever.

Thou coveredst it with the deep as with a garment: the waters stood above the mountains.

At thy rebuke they fled; at the voice of thy thunder they hasted away.

They go up by the mountains; they go down by the valleys unto the place which thou hast founded for them.

Thou hast set a bound that they may not pass over; that they turn not again to cover the earth.

He sendeth the springs into the valleys, which run among the hills.

They give drink to every beast of the field: the wild asses quench their thirst.

By them shall the fowls of the heaven have their habitation, which sing among the branches.

He watereth the hills from his chambers: the earth is satisfied with the fruit of thy works.

He causeth the grass to grow for the cattle, and herb for the service of man: that he may bring forth food out of the earth;

And wine that maketh glad the heart of man, and oil to make his face to shine, and bread which strengtheneth man's heart.

The trees of the Lord are full of sap; the cedars of Lebanon, which he hath planted;

Where the birds make their nests: as for the stork, the fir trees are her house.

The high hills are a refuge for the wild goats; and the rocks for the conies.

He appointed the moon for seasons: the sun knoweth his going down.

Thou makest darkness, and it is night: wherein all the beasts of the forest do creep forth.

The young lions roar after their prey, and seek their meat from God.

The sun ariseth, they gather themselves together, and lay them down in their dens.

Man goeth forth unto his work and to his labour until the evening.

O Lord, how manifold are thy works! in wisdom hast thou made them all: the earth is full of thy riches.

So is this great and wide sea, wherein are things creeping innumerable, both small and great beasts.

There go the ships: there is that leviathan, whom thou hast made to play therein.

These wait all upon thee; that thou mayest give them their meat in due season.

That thou givest them they gather: thou openest thine hand, they are filled with good.

Thou hidest thy face, they are troubled: thou takest away their breath, they die, and return to their dust.

Thou sendest forth thy spirit, they are created: and thou renewest the face of the earth.

The glory of the Lord shall endure for ever: the Lord shall rejoice in his works.

He looketh on the earth, and it trembleth: he toucheth the hills, and they smoke.

I will sing unto the Lord as long as I live: I will sing praise to my God while I have my being.

My meditation of him shall be sweet: I will be glad in the Lord.

Let the sinners be consumed out of the earth, and let the wicked be no more. Bless thou the Lord, O my soul. Praise ye the Lord.

PSALM 104

A PRAYER TO BE DELIVERED FROM LIARS AND WARMONGERS

In my distress I cried unto the Lord, and he heard me.

Deliver my soul, O Lord, from lying lips, and from a deceitful tongue.

What shall be given unto thee? or what shall be done unto thee, thou false tongue?

Sharp arrows of the mighty, with coals of juniper.

Woe is me, that I sojourn in Mesech, that I dwell in the tents of Kedar!

My soul hath long dwelt with him that hateth peace.

I am for peace: but when I speak, they are for war.

PSALM 120

A SONG OF THANKSGIVING

If it had not been the Lord who was on our side, now may Israel say;

If it had not been the Lord who was on our side, when men rose up against us:

Then they had swallowed us up quick, when their wrath was kindled against us:

Then the waters had overwhelmed us, the stream had gone over our soul:

Then the proud waters had gone over our soul.

Blessed be the Lord, who hath not given us as a prey to their teeth.

Our soul is escaped as a bird out of the snare of the fowlers: the snare is broken, and we are escaped.

Our help is in the name of the Lord, who made heaven and earth.

PSALM 124

THE LORD HATH DONE
GREAT THINGS FOR US

When the Lord turned again the captivity of Zion, we were like them that dream.

Then was our mouth filled with laughter, and our tongue with singing: then said they among the heathen, The Lord hath done great things for them.

The Lord hath done great things for us; whereof we are glad.

Turn again our captivity, O Lord, as the streams in the south.

They that sow in tears shall reap in joy.

He that goeth forth and weepeth, bearing precious seed, shall doubtless come again with rejoicing, bringing his sheaves with him.

PSALM 126

ON THE GIFTS OF GOD

Except the Lord build the house, they labour in vain that build it: except the Lord keep the city, the watchman waketh but in vain.

It is vain for you to rise up early, to sit up late, to eat the bread of sorrows: for so he giveth his beloved sleep.

Lo, children are an heritage of the Lord: and the fruit of the womb is his reward.

As arrows are in the hand of a mighty man; so are children of the youth.

Happy is the man that hath his quiver full of them: they shall not be ashamed, but they shall speak with the enemies in the gate.

PSALM 127

BY THE RIVERS OF BABYLON

By the rivers of Babylon, there we sat down, yea, we wept, when we remembered Zion.

We hanged our harps upon the willows in the midst thereof.

For there they that carried us away captive required of us a song; and they that wasted us required of us mirth, saying, Sing us one of the songs of Zion.

How shall we sing the Lord's song in a strange land?

If I forget thee, O Jerusalem, let my right hand forget her cunning.

If I do not remember thee, let my tongue cleave to the roof of my mouth; if I prefer not Jerusalem above my chief joy.

Remember, O Lord, the children of Edom in the day of Jerusalem; who said, Rase it, rase it, even to the foundation thereof.

O daughter of Babylon, who art to be destroyed; happy shall he be, that rewardeth thee as thou hast served us.

Happy shall he be, that taketh and dasheth thy little ones against the stones.

PSALM 137

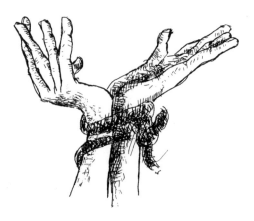

ALL THINGS COME ALIKE TO ALL

For all this I considered in my heart even to declare all this, that the righteous, and the wise, and their works, are in the hand of God: no man knoweth either love or hatred by all that is before them.

All things come alike to all: there is one event to the righteous, and to the wicked; to the good and to the clean, and to the unclean; to him that sacrificeth, and to him that sacrificeth not: as is the good, so is the sinner; and he that sweareth, as he that feareth an oath.

This is an evil among all things that are done under the sun, that there is one event unto all: yea, also the heart of the sons of men is full of evil, and madness is in their heart while they live, and after that they go to the dead.

For to him that is joined to all the living there is hope: for a living dog is better than a dead lion.

For the living know that they shall die: but the dead know not any thing, neither have they any more a reward; for the memory of them is forgotten.

Also their love, and their hatred, and their envy, is now perished; neither have they any more a portion for ever in any thing that is done under the sun.

Go thy way, eat thy bread with joy, and drink thy wine with a merry heart; for God now accepteth thy works.

Let thy garments be always white; and let thy head lack no ointment.

Live joyfully with the wife whom thou lovest all the days of the life of thy vanity, which he hath given thee under the sun, all the days of thy vanity: for that is thy portion in this life, and in thy labour which thou takest under the sun.

Whatsoever thy hand findeth to do, do it with thy might; for there is no work, nor device, nor knowledge, nor wisdom, in the grave, whither thou goest.

I returned, and saw under the sun, that the race is not to the swift, nor the battle to the strong, neither yet bread to the wise, nor yet riches to men of understanding, nor yet favour to men of skill; but time and chance happeneth to them all.

For man also knoweth not his time: as the fishes that are taken in an evil net, and as the birds that are caught in the snare; so are the sons of men snared in an evil time, when it falleth suddenly upon them.

ECCLESIASTES 9:1–12

REMEMBER NOW THY CREATOR

Remember now thy Creator in the days of thy youth, while the evil days come not, nor the years draw nigh, when thou shalt say, I have no pleasure in them;

While the sun, or the light, or the moon, or the stars, be not darkened, nor the clouds return after the rain:

In the day when the keepers of the house shall tremble, and the strong men shall bow themselves, and the grinders cease because they are few, and those that look out of the windows be darkened,

And the doors shall be shut in the streets, when the sound of the grinding is low, and he shall rise up at the voice of the bird, and all the daughters of music shall be brought low;

Also when they shall be afraid of that which is high, and fears shall be in the way, and the almond tree shall flourish, and the grasshopper shall be a burden, and desire shall fail: because man goeth to his long home, and the mourners go about the streets:

Or ever the silver cord be loosed, or the golden bowl be broken, or the pitcher be broken at the fountain, or the wheel broken at the cistern.

Then shall the dust return to the earth as it was: and the spirit shall return unto God who gave it.

ECCLESIASTES 12:1–7

ARISE, MY LOVE

I am the rose of Sharon, and the lily of the valleys.

As the lily among thorns, so is my love among the daughters.

As the apple tree among the trees of the wood, so is my beloved among the sons. I sat down under his shadow with great delight, and his fruit was sweet to my taste.

He brought me to the banqueting house, and his banner over me was love.

Stay me with flagons, comfort me with apples: for I am sick of love.

His left hand is under my head, and his right hand doth embrace me.

I charge you, O ye daughters of Jerusalem, by the roes, and by the hinds of the field, that ye stir not up, nor awake my love, till he please.

The voice of my beloved! behold, he cometh leaping upon the mountains, skipping upon the hills.

My beloved is like a roe or a young hart: behold, he standeth behind our wall, he looketh forth at the windows, shewing himself through the lattice.

My beloved spake, and said unto me, Rise up, my love, my fair one, and come away.

For, lo, the winter is past, the rain is over and gone;

The flowers appear on the earth; the time of the singing of birds is come, and the voice of the turtle is heard in our land;

The fig tree putteth forth her green figs, and the vines with the tender grape give a good smell. Arise, my love, my fair one, and come away.

O my dove, that art in the clefts of the rock, in the secret places of the stairs, let me see thy countenance, let me hear thy voice; for sweet is thy voice, and thy countenance is comely.

Take us the foxes, the little foxes, that spoil the vines: for our vines have tender grapes.

My beloved is mine, and I am his: he feedeth among the lilies.

Until the day break, and the shadows flee away, turn, my beloved, and be thou like a roe or a young hart upon the mountains of Bether.

THE SONG OF SOLOMON 2

BEHOLD, THOU ART FAIR, MY LOVE

Behold, thou art fair, my love; behold, thou art fair; thou hast doves' eyes within thy locks: thy hair is as a flock of goats, that appear from mount Gilead.

Thy teeth are like a flock of sheep that are even shorn, which came up from the washing; whereof every one bear twins, and none is barren among them.

Thy lips are like a thread of scarlet, and thy speech is comely: thy temples are like a piece of a pomegranate within thy locks.

Thy neck is like the tower of David builded for an armoury, whereon there hang a thousand bucklers, all shields of mighty men.

Thy two breasts are like two young roes that are twins, which feed among the lilies.

Until the day break, and the shadows flee away, I will get me to the mountain of myrrh, and to the hill of frankincense.

Thou art all fair, my love; there is no spot in thee.

Come with me from Lebanon, my spouse, with me from Lebanon: look from the top of Amana, from the top of Shenir and Hermon, from the lions' dens, from the mountains of the leopards.

Thou hast ravished my heart, my sister, my spouse; thou hast ravished my heart with one of thine eyes, with one chain of thy neck.

How fair is thy love, my sister, my spouse! how much better is thy love than wine! and the smell of thine ointments than all spices!

Thy lips, O my spouse, drop as the honeycomb: honey and milk are under thy tongue; and the smell of thy garments is like the smell of Lebanon.

A garden inclosed is my sister, my spouse; a spring shut up, a fountain sealed.

Thy plants are an orchard of pomegranates, with pleasant fruits; camphire, with spikenard,

Spikenard and saffron; calamus and cinnamon, with all trees of frankincense; myrrh and aloes, with all the chief spices:

A fountain of gardens, a well of living waters, and streams from Lebanon.

Awake, O north wind; and come, thou south; blow upon my garden, that the spices thereof may flow out. Let my beloved come into his garden, and eat his pleasant fruits.

THE SONG OF SOLOMON 4

HOW BEAUTIFUL ARE
THY FEET WITH SHOES

How beautiful are thy feet with shoes, O prince's daughter! the joints of thy thighs are like jewels, the work of the hands of a cunning workman.

Thy navel is like a round goblet, which wanteth not liquor: thy belly is like an heap of wheat set about with lilies.

Thy two breasts are like two young roes that are twins.

Thy neck is as a tower of ivory; thine eyes like the fishpools in Heshbon, by the gate of Bathrabbim: thy nose is as the tower of Lebanon which looketh toward Damascus.

Thine head upon thee is like Carmel, and the hair of thine head like purple; the king is held in the galleries.

How fair and how pleasant art thou, O love, for delights!

This thy stature is like to a palm tree, and thy breasts to clusters of grapes.

I said, I will go up to the palm tree, I will take hold of the boughs thereof: now also thy breasts shall be as clusters of the vine, and the smell of thy nose like apples;

And the roof of thy mouth like the best wine for my beloved, that goeth down sweetly, causing the lips of those that are asleep to speak.

I am my beloved's, and his desire is toward me.

Come, my beloved, let us go forth into the field; let us lodge in the villages.

Let us get up early to the vineyards; let us see if the vine flourish, whether the tender grape appear, and the pomegranates bud forth: there will I give thee my loves.

The mandrakes give a smell, and at our gates are all manner of pleasant fruits, new and old, which I have laid up for thee, O my beloved.

THE SONG OF SOLOMON 7

THE FIRE OF LOVE

O that thou wert as my brother, that sucked the breasts of my mother! when I should find thee without, I would kiss thee; yea, I should not be despised.

I would lead thee, and bring thee into my mother's house, who would instruct me: I would cause thee to drink of spiced wine of the juice of my pomegranate.

His left hand should be under my head, and his right hand should embrace me.

I charge you, O daughters of Jerusalem, that ye stir not up, nor awake my love, until he please.

Who is this that cometh up from the wilderness, leaning upon her beloved? I raised thee up under the apple tree: there thy mother brought thee forth: there she brought thee forth that bare thee.

Set me as a seal upon thine heart, as a seal upon thine arm: for love is strong as death; jealousy is cruel as the grave: the coals thereof are coals of fire, which hath a most vehement flame.

Many waters cannot quench love, neither can the floods drown it: if a man would give all the substance of his house for love, it would utterly be contemned.

We have a little sister, and she hath no breasts: what shall we do for our sister in the day when she shall be spoken for?

If she be a wall, we will build upon her a palace of silver: and if she be a door, we will inclose her with boards of cedar.

I am a wall, and my breasts like towers: then was I in his eyes as one that found favour.

Solomon had a vineyard at Baalhamon; he let out the vineyard unto keepers; every one for the fruit thereof was to bring a thousand pieces of silver.

My vineyard, which is mine, is before me: thou, O Solomon, must have a thousand, and those that keep the fruit thereof two hundred.

Thou that dwellest in the gardens, the companions hearken to thy voice: cause me to hear it.

Make haste, my beloved, and be thou like to a roe or to a young hart upon the mountains of spices.

THE SONG OF SOLOMON 8

FROM THE PROPHECY AGAINST EGYPT

Where are they? where are thy wise men? and let them tell thee now, and let them know what the Lord of hosts hath pur-. posed upon Egypt.

The princes of Zoan are become fools, the princes of Noph are deceived; they have also seduced Egypt, even they that are the stay of the tribes thereof.

The Lord hath mingled a perverse spirit in the midst thereof: and they have caused Egypt to err in every work thereof, as a drunken man staggereth in his vomit.

Neither shall there be any work for Egypt, which the head or tail, branch or rush, may do.

In that day shall Egypt be like unto women: and it shall be afraid and fear because of the shaking of the hand of the Lord of hosts, which he shaketh over it.

And the land of Judah shall be a terror unto Egypt, every one that maketh mention thereof shall be afraid in himself, because of the counsel of the Lord of hosts, which he hath determined against it.

In that day shall five cities in the land of Egypt speak the language of Canaan, and swear to the Lord of hosts; one shall be called, The city of destruction.

In that day shall there be an altar to the Lord in the midst of the land of Egypt, and a pillar at the border thereof to the Lord.

And it shall be for a sign and for a witness unto the Lord of hosts in the land of Egypt: for they shall cry unto the Lord because of the oppressors, and he shall send them a saviour, and a great one, and he shall deliver them.

And the Lord shall be known to Egypt, and the Egyptians shall know the Lord in that day, and shall do sacrifice and oblation; yea, they shall vow a vow unto the Lord, and perform it.

And the Lord shall smite Egypt: he shall smite and heal it: and they shall return even to the Lord, and he shall be intreated of them, and shall heal them.

In that day shall there be a highway out of Egypt to Assyria, and the Assyrian shall come into Egypt, and the Egyptian into Assyria, and the Egyptians shall serve with the Assyrians.

In that day shall Israel be the third with Egypt and with Assyria, even a blessing in the midst of the land:

Whom the Lord of hosts shall bless, saying, Blessed be Egypt my people, and Assyria the work of my hands, and Israel mine inheritance.

Isaiah 19:12–25

THE WRITING OF HEZEKIAH KING OF JUDAH, WHEN HE HAD BEEN SICK, AND WAS RECOVERED OF HIS SICKNESS

I said in the cutting off of my days, I shall go to the gates of the grave: I am deprived of the residue of my years.

I said, I shall not see the Lord, even the Lord, in the land of the living: I shall behold man no more with the inhabitants of the world.

Mine age is departed, and is removed from me as a shepherd's tent: I have cut off like a weaver my life: he will cut me off with pining sickness: from day even to night wilt thou make an end of me.

I reckoned till morning, that, as a lion, so will he break all my bones: from day even to night wilt thou make an end of me.

Like a crane or a swallow, so did I chatter: I did mourn as a dove: mine eyes fail with looking upward: O Lord, I am oppressed; undertake for me.

What shall I say? he hath both spoken unto me, and himself hath done it: I shall go softly all my years in the bitterness of my soul.

O Lord, by these things men live, and in all these things is the life of my spirit: so wilt thou recover me, and make me to live.

Behold, for peace I had great bitterness: but thou hast in love to my soul delivered it from the pit of corruption: for thou hast cast all my sins behind thy back.

For the grave cannot praise thee, death can not celebrate thee: they that go down into the pit cannot hope for thy truth.

The living, the living, he shall praise thee, as I do this day: the father to the children shall make known thy truth.

The Lord was ready to save me: therefore we will sing my songs to the stringed instruments all the days of our life in the house of the Lord.

Isaiah 38:10–20

THE INVITATION

Ho, every one that thirsteth, come ye to the waters, and he that hath no money; come ye, buy, and eat; yea, come, buy wine and milk without money and without price.

Wherefore do ye spend money for that which is not bread? and your labour for that which satisfieth not? hearken diligently unto me, and eat ye that which is good, and let your soul delight itself in fatness.

Incline your ear, and come unto me: hear, and your soul shall live; and I will make an everlasting covenant with you, even the sure mercies of David.

Behold, I have given him for a witness to the people, a leader and commander to the people.

Behold, thou shalt call a nation that thou knowest not, and nations that knew not thee shall run unto thee because of the Lord thy God, and for the Holy One of Israel; for he hath glorified thee.

Seek ye the Lord while he may be found, call ye upon him while he is near:

Let the wicked forsake his way, and the unrighteous man his thoughts: and let him return unto the Lord, and he will have mercy upon him, and to our God, for he will abundantly pardon.

For my thoughts are not your thoughts, neither are your ways my ways, saith the Lord.

For as the heavens are higher than the earth, so are my ways higher than your ways, and my thoughts than your thoughts.

For as the rain cometh down, and the snow from heaven, and returneth not thither, but watereth the earth, and maketh it bring forth and bud, that it may give seed to the sower, and bread to the eater:

So shall my word be that goeth forth out of my mouth: it shall not return unto me void, but it shall accomplish that which I please, and it shall prosper in the thing whereto I sent it.

For ye shall go out with joy, and be led forth with peace: the mountains and the hills shall break forth before you into singing, and all the trees of the field shall clap their hands.

Instead of the thorn shall come up the fir tree, and instead of the brier shall come up the myrtle tree: and it shall be to the Lord for a name, for an everlasting sign that shall not be cut off.

Isaiah 55

REJOICE NOT, O ISRAEL, FOR JOY

Rejoice not, O Israel, for joy, as other people: for thou hast gone a whoring from thy God, thou hast loved a reward upon every cornfloor.

The floor and the winepress shall not feed them, and the new wine shall fail in her.

They shall not dwell in the Lord's land; but Ephraim shall return to Egypt, and they shall eat unclean things in Assyria.

They shall not offer wine offerings to the Lord, neither shall they be pleasing unto him: their sacrifices shall be unto them as the bread of mourners; all that eat thereof shall be polluted: for their bread for their soul shall not come into the house of the Lord.

What will ye do in the solemn day, and in the day of the feast of the Lord?

For, lo, they are gone because of destruction: Egypt shall gather them up, Memphis shall bury them: the pleasant places for their silver, nettles shall possess them: thorns shall be in their tabernacles.

The days of visitation are come, the days of recompense are come; Israel shall know it: the prophet is a fool, the spiritual man is mad, for the multitude of thine iniquity, and the great hatred.

The watchman of Ephraim was with my God: but the prophet is a snare of a fowler in all his ways, and hatred in the house of his God.

They have deeply corrupted themselves, as in the days of Gibeah: therefore he will remember their iniquity, he will visit their sins.

I found Israel like grapes in the wilderness; I saw your fathers as the first ripe in the fig tree at her first time: but they went to Baal-peor, and separated themselves unto that shame; and their abominations were according as they loved.

As for Ephraim, their glory shall fly away like a bird, from the birth, and from the womb, and from the conception.

Though they bring up their children, yet will I bereave them, that there shall not be a man left: yea, woe also to them when I depart from them!

Ephraim, as I saw Tyrus, is planted in a pleasant place: but Ephraim shall bring forth his children to the murderer.

Give them, O Lord: what wilt thou give? give them a miscarrying womb and dry breasts.

All their wickedness is in Gilgal: for there I hated them: for the wickedness of their doings I will drive them out of mine house, I will love them no more: all their princes are revolters.

Ephraim is smitten, their root is dried up, they shall bear no fruit: yea, though they bring forth, yet will I slay even the beloved fruit of their womb.

My God will cast them away, because they did not hearken unto him: and they shall be wanderers among the nations.

HOSEA 9

THE PROPHECIES AGAINST MOAB, JUDAH, AND ISRAEL

Thus saith the Lord; For three transgressions of Moab, and for four, I will not turn away the punishment thereof; because he burned the bones of the king of Edom into lime:

But I will send a fire upon Moab, and it shall devour the palaces of Kirioth: and Moab shall die with tumult, with shouting, and with the sound of the trumpet:

And I will cut off the judge from the midst thereof, and will slay all the princes thereof with him, saith the Lord.

Thus saith the Lord; For three transgressions of Judah, and for four, I will not turn away the punishment thereof; because they have despised the law of the Lord, and have not kept his commandments, and their lies caused them to err, after the which their fathers have walked:

But I will send a fire upon Judah, and it shall devour the palaces of Jerusalem.

Thus saith the Lord; For three transgressions of Israel, and for four, I will not turn away the punishment thereof; because they sold the righteous for silver, and the poor for a pair of shoes;

That pant after the dust of the earth on the head of the poor, and turn aside the way of the meek: and a man and his father will go in unto the same maid, to profane my holy name:

And they lay themselves down upon clothes laid to pledge by every altar, and they drink the wine of the condemned in the house of their god.

Yet destroyed I the Amorite before them, whose height was like the height of the cedars, and he was strong as the oaks; yet I destroyed his fruit from above, and his roots from beneath.

Also I brought you up from the land of Egypt, and led you forty years through the wilderness, to possess the land of the Amorite.

And I raised up of your sons for prophets, and of your young men for Nazarites. Is it not even thus, O ye children of Israel? saith the Lord.

But ye gave the Nazarites wine to drink; and commanded the prophets, saying, Prophesy not.

Behold, I am pressed under you, as a cart is pressed that is full of sheaves.

Therefore the flight shall perish from the swift, and the strong shall not strengthen his force, neither shall the mighty deliver himself:

Neither shall he stand that handleth the bow; and he that is swift of foot shall not deliver himself: neither shall he that rideth the horse deliver himself.

And he that is courageous among the mighty shall flee away naked in that day, saith the Lord.

AMOS 2

THE BASKET OF SUMMER FRUIT

Thus hath the Lord God shewed unto me: and behold a basket of summer fruit.

And he said, Amos, what seest thou? And I said, A basket of summer fruit. Then said the Lord unto me, The end is come upon my people of Israel; I will not again pass by them any more.

And the songs of the temple shall be howlings in that day, saith the Lord God: there shall be many dead bodies in every place; they shall cast them forth with silence.

Hear this, O ye that swallow up the needy, even to make the poor of the land to fail,

Saying, When will the new moon be gone, that we may sell corn? and the sabbath, that we may set forth wheat, making the ephah small, and the shekel great, and falsifying the balances by deceit?

That we may buy the poor for silver, and the needy for a pair of shoes; yea, and sell the refuse of the wheat?

The Lord hath sworn by the excellency of Jacob, Surely I will never forget any of their works.

Shall not the land tremble for this, and every one mourn that dwelleth therein? and it shall rise up wholly as a flood; and it shall be cast out and drowned, as by the flood of Egypt.

And it shall come to pass in that day, saith the Lord God, that I will cause the sun to go down at noon, and I will darken the earth in the clear day:

And I will turn your feasts into mourning, and all your songs into lamentation; and I will bring up sackcloth upon all loins, and baldness upon every head; and I will make it as the mourning of an only son, and the end thereof as a bitter day.

Behold, the days come, saith the Lord God, that I will send a famine in the land, not a famine of bread, nor a thirst for water, but of hearing the words of the Lord:

And they shall wander from sea to sea, and from the north even to the east, they shall run to and fro to seek the word of the Lord, and shall not find it.

In that day shall the fair virgins and young men faint for thirst.

They that swear by the sin of Samaria, and say, Thy god, O Dan, liveth; and, The manner of Beersheba liveth: even they shall fall, and never rise up again.

AMOS 8

A DENUNCIATION OF
THE PRINCES AND PROPHETS

And I said, Hear, I pray you, O heads of Jacob, and ye princes of the house of Israel; Is it not for you to know judgment?

Who hate the good, and love the evil; who pluck off their skin from off them, and their flesh from off their bones;

Who also eat the flesh of my people, and flay their skin from off them; and they break their bones, and chop them in pieces, as for the pot, and as flesh within the caldron.

Then shall they cry unto the Lord, but he will not hear them: he will even hide his face from them at that time, as they have behaved themselves ill in their doings.

Thus saith the Lord concerning the prophets that make my people err, that bite with their teeth, and cry, Peace; and he that putteth not into their mouths, they even prepare war against him.

Therefore night shall be unto you, that ye shall not have a vision; and it shall be dark unto you, that ye shall not divine; and the sun shall go down over the prophets, and the day shall be dark over them.

Then shall the seers be ashamed, and the diviners confounded: yea, they shall all cover their lips; for there is no answer of God.

But truly I am full of power by the spirit of the Lord, and of judgment, and of might, to declare unto Jacob his transgression, and to Israel his sin.

Hear this, I pray you, ye heads of the house of Jacob, and princes of the house of Israel, that abhor judgment, and pervert all equity.

They build up Zion with blood, and Jerusalem with iniquity.

The heads thereof judge for reward, and the priests thereof teach for hire, and the prophets thereof divine for money: yet will they lean upon the Lord, and say, Is not the Lord among us? none evil can come upon us.

Therefore shall Zion for your sake be plowed as a field, and Jerusalem shall become heaps, and the mountain of the house as the high places of the forest.

MICAH 3

JUDGMENT AND SUNRISE

For, behold, the day cometh, that shall burn as an oven; and all the proud, yea, and all that do wickedly, shall be stubble: and the day that cometh shall burn them up, saith the Lord of hosts, that it shall leave them neither root nor branch.

But unto you that fear my name shall the Sun of righteousness arise with healing in his wings; and ye shall go forth, and grow up as calves of the stall.

And ye shall tread down the wicked; for they shall be ashes under the soles of your feet in the day that I shall do this, saith the Lord of hosts.

Remember ye the law of Moses my servant, which I commanded unto him in Horeb for all Israel, with the statutes and judgments.

Behold, I will send you Elijah the prophet before the coming of the great and dreadful day of the Lord:

And he shall turn the heart of the fathers to the children, and the heart of the children to their fathers, lest I come and smite the earth with a curse.

MALACHI 4

The Poets of

MOORISH SPAIN

You are a servant of the living
God. Why have you enslaved
yourself to the earth?

—ABRAHAM IBN EZRA

WAR

War at first is like a young girl
With whom every man desires to flirt.
And at the last it is an old woman,
All who meet her feel grieved and hurt.

SAMUEL THE PRINCE
Translated by David Goldstein

HIS ANSWER TO THE CRITICS

Where are the men with the strength to be men?
Where are those who have eyes and can see?
Looking around, I see nothing but cowards and cynics,
And slaves, slaves to their own senses.
And every one of these poor beggars
Thinks of himself as another Aristotle.
You tell me they have written poems—
You call that poetry?
I call it the cawing of crows.
It's time for the prophet's anger to purify poetry,
Left too long to the fingers of aesthetes and time-wasters.
I have carved my song in the high forehead of Time.
They know it and hate it—it is too much.

SOLOMON IBN GABIROL
Translated by Robert Mezey

AN APPLE FOR ISAAC

My lord, take this delicacy in your hand.
Smell its fragrance. Forget your longing.
On both sides it blushes, like a young girl
At the first touch of my hand on her breast.
It is an orphan, with no brother, no sister,
Far away from its leafy home.
When it was plucked, its companions were jealous,
They envied its journey, and cried:
"Bear greetings to your master, Isaac.
How lucky you are to be kissed by his lips!"

SOLOMON IBN GABIROL
Translated by David Goldstein

IN THE MORNING I LOOK FOR YOU

In the morning I look for you,
My rock and my tower.
I lay my prayers before you,
That, day and night, are in me.

I stand before your greatness
And am unnerved,
Because your eye will see
The thoughts that are in me.

What is it that the heart
Or the tongue can do,
And what power is there
In the spirit that is in me?

But I know that you are pleased
With the songs that men make,
And so I will sing to you
While the breath is in me.

SOLOMON IBN GABIROL
Translated by David Goldstein

GRAVES

And where are the graves, so many graves
Of all who have died on the earth since the beginning?
Grave tunnelling into grave,
Headstone and obelisk crumbled into one dust,
Bodies heaped upon bodies, in motionless orgy—
All sleeping together in deep holes,
Fragments of chalk,
Stained rubies.

MOSES IBN EZRA
Translated by Robert Mezey

TO MOSES IBN EZRA,
IN CHRISTIAN SPAIN

How, after you, can I find rest?
You go and my heart goes with you.
Were I not to wait for the day of your return,
Your departure would have made my death complete.
Look, the mountains of Bether testify
That the clouds are miserly and my tears abundant.
Return to the West, lamp of the West.
Become a seal on every heart and hand.
Why with your pure lips do you linger among stammerers?
Why does the dew of Hermon settle on Gilboa?

JUDAH HALEVI
Translated by David Goldstein

MOUNT AVARIM

Shalom, Mount Avarim. Blessed be your slopes.
Somewhere on you the greatest of men was gathered,
Sacred bones now buried deep in your side.
If you do not know him, ask the Red Sea,
Ask the green bush, ask Sinai, and they will tell you:
"He was not a man of words, but he did God's work."
I have vowed to visit you soon, God willing.

JUDAH HALEVI
Translated by Robert Mezey

MY HEART IS IN THE EAST

My heart is in the East, and I in the uttermost West—
My food has no taste, there is no sweetness in it.
How can I keep the faith while Zion lies
Under Edom's foot and I in the chains of the Arab?
I would leave in a minute this Spain and all its pleasures—
I would give anything to walk just once
The ruined and empty courts of the Sanctuary.

JUDAH HALEVI
Translated by Robert Mezey

JERUSALEM

Beautiful heights, city of a great King,
From the western coast my desire burns towards thee.
Pity and tenderness burst in me, remembering
Thy former glories, thy temple now broken stones.
I wish I could fly to thee on the wings of an eagle
And mingle my tears with thy dust.
I have sought thee, love, though the King is not there
And instead of Gilead's balm, snakes and scorpions.
Let me fall on thy broken stones and tenderly kiss them—
The taste of thy dust will be sweeter than honey to me.

JUDAH HALEVI
Translated by Robert Mezey

THE APPLE

You have enslaved me with your lovely body;
You have put me in a kind of prison.
Since the day we parted,
I have found nothing that is like your beauty.
So I comfort myself with a ripe apple—
Its fragrance reminds me of the myrrh of your breath,
Its shape of your breasts, its color
Of the color that used to rise to your cheeks.

JUDAH HALEVI
Translated by Robert Mezey

CUPS WITHOUT WINE

Cups without wine are low things
Like a pot thrown to the ground,
But brimming with the juice, they shine
Like body and soul.

JUDAH HALEVI
Translated by Robert Mezey

A SECRET KEPT

A girl brought me into the house of love,
A girl as pure and perfect as Abigail,
And taking off her clothes, she revealed a body
So dazzling, it beggared comparison.
Her light shining in the darkness made everything tremble,
The hills began dancing like rams.
"O Lord," I thought, "our secrets will be discovered,"
But she reached back at once with her powerful hands
And covered us both with her long black hair,
And once again it was night.

JUDAH AL-HARIZI
Translated by Robert Mezey

MY STARS

On the day I was born,
The unalterable stars altered.
If I decided to sell lamps,
It wouldn't get dark till the day I died.

Some stars. Whatever I do,
I'm a failure before I begin.
If I suddenly decided to sell shrouds,
People would suddenly stop dying.

ABRAHAM IBN EZRA
Translated by Robert Mezey

BORN WITHOUT A STAR

I come in the morn
To the house of the nobly born.
They say he rode away.
I come again at the end of day,
But he is not at his best
And he needs rest.
He is always either sleeping or riding afar.
Woe to the man who is born without a star.

ABRAHAM IBN EZRA
Translated by Meyer Waxman

I HAVE A GARMENT

I have a garment which is like a sieve
Through which girls sift barley and wheat.
In the dead of night I spread it out like a tent
And a thousand stars pierce it with their gleams.
Sitting inside, I see the moon and the Pleiades
And on a good night, the great Orion himself.
I get awfully tired of counting all the holes
Which seem to me like the teeth of many saws.
A piece of thread to sew up all the other threads
Would be, to say the least, superfluous.
If a fly landed on it with all his weight,
The little idiot would hang by his foot, cursing.
Dear God, do what you can to mend it.
Make me a mantle of praise from these poor rags.

ABRAHAM IBN EZRA
Translated by Robert Mezey

O LORD, SAVE WE BESEECH THEE

O Lord, save we beseech Thee.
O Lord, prosper we beseech Thee.
O Lord, answer us on the day that we call.

God of spirits, save we beseech Thee.
Searcher of hearts, prosper we beseech Thee.
O strong Redeemer, answer us on the day that we call.

Utterer of righteousness, save we beseech Thee.
Clothed in glory, prosper we beseech Thee.
Omnipotent and gracious, answer us on the day that we call.

Pure and upright, save we beseech Thee.
Thou who pitiest the poor, prosper we beseech Thee.
Good and bountiful Lord, answer us on the day that we call.

Diviner of thoughts, save we beseech Thee.
Mighty and resplendent, prosper we beseech Thee.
Thou that are clothed in righteousness, answer us on the day that
    we call.

King of the worlds, save we beseech Thee.
Girdled with light and majesty, prosper we beseech Thee.
Thou who supportest the falling, answer us on the day that we
    call.

Helper of the poor, save we beseech Thee.
Redeemer and Deliverer, prosper we beseech Thee.
O everlasting Rock, answer us on the day that we call.

Holy and revered, save we beseech Thee.
Merciful and compassionate, prosper we beseech Thee.
Keeper of the Covenant, answer us on the day that we call.

Stay of the perfect, save we beseech Thee.
Eternal Sovereign, prosper we beseech Thee.
Thou that art perfect in all Thy ways, O answer us on the day
    that we call.

ANONYMOUS
Translated by H. M. Adler

The

MODERN POETS

Our body is very wild. It is a
wandering body of symbols.
And is our nervous system in
any way like that of the
Gentiles? The Hebrew mouth is
more like a wound; behind the
Hebrew forehead an eagle
screams.

—URI ZVI GREENBERG

TWILIGHT PIECE

Up rose the sun again, again the sun set.
I didn't see.
Day followed day followed day, but not one note
From the sky for me.

Upon the western rim, the piled-up clouds again,
Hulk on hulk, blazed.
Sages—what worlds are rising here?
What worlds being razed?

No worlds are rising there; no worlds are razed.
I only see
Imbecile evening scattering ashes
On the earth and the sea.

"I looked for your penny but I lost my crown,"
That's what I see within,
While Mephistopheles stands behind me
Grinning his cruel grin.

CHAIM NACHMAN BIALIK
Translated by Robert Friend

O THOU SEER, GO, FLEE THEE AWAY
(Amos 7:12)

Flee thee away? A man like myself doesn't flee.
Walk on by is what my cattle taught me.
But my tongue never did learn to walk that way
And my words come down like an ax.

It's not my fault if my strength was spent in vain,
Don't blame me, blame yourself.
My hammer found no anvil under it,
My ax sank deep into rotten wood.

Let it go. I make peace with my fate.
Day laborer, working for no pay,
I'll tie my tools to my belt
And quietly go back the way I came,

Back to my own country and its valleys,
And make a pact with the forest sycamores.
As for you—rot, filth, everything that is dying,
Tomorrow the storm will carry you all away.

CHAIM NACHMAN BIALIK
Translated by Robert Mezey and Shula Starkman

ALONE

The wind took them, light swept them all away,
The morning of their lives sang with a new sense,
While I, a soft fledgling, remained below
The wing of God's presence.

I was left utterly alone, and the Presence
Fluttered above my head her smashed right wing.
My heart knew her heart, she trembled
On her son, her only one.

She was driven away from everywhere.
Only one small grim lonely place was left:
The house of study where she hid in shadow
And I shared her grief.

When my heart yearned for the window, for the light,
When I grew embittered at her wing's hard weight,
She laid her head on my shoulder, her tears dripped
On the pages of the Talmud.

She wept to me softly and clung to me
As though I was enclosed by her smashed wing,
"The wind took them, they all grew and blossomed,
I stayed alone."

And like the closing of an old lament,
Like a prayer moving in pleading and in fear,
My ear listened to that gentle weeping
And to that scalding tear . . .

CHAIM NACHMAN BIALIK
Translated by A. C. Jacobs

ON SLAUGHTER

Heaven, ask pity for me!
If God still lives there,
if there is still a path,
if I don't find it,
you pray for me.
As for me, my heart died some time back;
there is no more prayer on my lips;
my hands lie useless
and I live without hope.
How much longer? How much?

Executioner, here is a throat—
get up and cut it!
Break my neck like a dog's.
You have an arm and an ax,
and to me the whole earth is a scaffold.
And we, we are few.
Free blood! Crush a skull
and watch the murder juice leap out!
There's an old man and a suckling on your shirt,
which will never be white again.

If there is justice, let it appear at once!
If it appears
only when I am nothing under the sun—
let its throne be thrown down and shattered!
Throughout eternities of guilt
let the heavens rot!
And you, you proud pigs,
be what you are.
Suck on your own blood,
live on it!

And damn the one who calls for vengeance!
Vengeance for this,
vengeance for the blood of a little boy—
the devil hasn't invented it.
Let the blood seep down through the abyss,
let the blood pierce to the floor of darkness,
and eat in darkness,
and undermine
all the rotting foundations of the earth!

CHAIM NACHMAN BIALIK
Translated by Robert Mezey and Shula Starkman

MAN IS NOTHING BUT

Man is nothing but the soil of a small country,
nothing but the shape of his native landscape,
nothing but what his ears recorded
when they were new and really heard,
what his eyes saw, before they had their fill of seeing—
everything a wondering child comes across
on the dew-softened paths,
stumbling over every lump of earth, every old stone,
while in a hidden place in his soul, unknown to him,
there's an altar set up
from which the smoke of his sacrifice rises each day
to the kingdom of the sky, to the stars,
to the houses of the Zodiac.
But when the days become many, and in the war of being
the scroll of his Book of Life is being interpreted—
then comes, one by one, each letter with its interpretation
and each symbol revealing past and future
that was inscribed in it when it was first opened.
A man is nothing but the landscape of his homeland.

And in that corner of earth where I was born,
in the vastness of the blue steppes,
the high places dreamed, the holy places,
on the backs of strange graves.
Nobody knows who spilled that earth, nobody knows when,
or who it is that sleeps for good in their laps.
And idols shrouded by the dust of many jubilees
look toward the mute grey borders,
like the steppes themselves before rain,
like the end of August when the earth cracks open
in a thousand places.
Kingdoms blossom and kingdoms sink into death

and the borders of states grow blurred and then sharp—
here on their beds they stand like headstones
on the back of a strange great past, forgotten forever,
faded away even out of poems and legends.

In that corner of earth where I was born
live the eagles of the field, lonely ones of the steppes,
giants with heavy wings and brown feathers,
like the sheaves of wheat the reapers left behind,
burnt by the east winds and eaten by heat and rain.
It happens sometimes that one comes down from the sky
and alights at the branching of roads, folding his wings—
a man will draw nearer and nearer
and then stop, and keeping his distance, stare at him.
And in his heart he will think: "What is this?
There is a sheaf and not a sheaf,
a bird and not a bird . . ."
When the eagle describes his pure God-circles in the sky
and hurls down from those heights his wild cry,
who will understand him? And who will know
why a bird calls out? Is it some kind of sigh,
or is it his song, childless,
without a listening heart, without an echo?
That cry is so lonely . . . dying over the steppes . . .

In that corner of earth where I was born,
there's an eternal fugitive;
there isn't a field he hasn't gone across,
no road he hasn't stumbled on
or come to the end of.
From the wing of earth to the wing of earth
he rushes and passes by. Do you know what I mean?
It's the wind! Sometimes he drives clouds as heavy as lead,
and sometimes he goes wild in open space,

sometimes he chases dust till it darkens the sun
and sometimes exults among the treasures of ice and snow.
And there is nothing, he thinks, to stop him
and no one who can stand in his way.
But when he turns his face to the south . . . to the south,
longing to reach the southern seas,
the ancient cliffs and mountains suddenly
stand in his way.

And so in the shape of that corner where I was born,
my life's history was spelled out to me
and my fate was revealed.
I worked my dream in a semblance of its own image:
with a free soul, free of stain or tatter,
with a whole heart all its strings speaking in harmony,
I wandered alone in the congregation of my people,
bowed beneath the blessing
and the curse of the big graves.
And my poem is a stranger, an alien
in the heart of my nation, lonely,
lonely, coming lonely and going lonely,
without a listening heart, without an echo,
a savage cry ringing in solitude.
And like the wind that goes wandering forever,
I wandered from ocean to ocean all the days of my life,
but when I had to get to the southern seas,
mountains rose up before me and blocked my way . . .
And where shall I build my nest?

More open space, more roads! Give me my stick.
I am going.

SAUL TCHERNICHOVSKY
Translated by Robert Mezey and Shula Starkman

THE GRAVE

In memory of those fallen in the Ukraine

There are many like him here, without epitaph, without a mound.
The ox pulling a plough stumbles on him,
The peasant behind the plough swears at him furiously,
And his clearing will be the shelter of the locust.

The field, before autumn—and only a cloud weeps for him
With cold cries. A storm silences it
And thus he is mourned. No one to say Kaddish.
The path bends around him and does not cry, O father!

Even this year, look, his land is becoming green,
Awakening from sleep and turning its burned face,
Aftergrowth bursting up from everywhere,
And the stalks of wheat mock him with sighing and scraping.

And this fellow, struck down by fire, decaying in the soot,
He doesn't know why the spade dug him a furrow,
Nor why he lived his painful life,
Nor why he was cut down and thrown here before his time.

SAUL TCHERNICHOVSKY
Translated by Robert Mezey and Shula Starkman

YOUR PEOPLE
ARE DROWNING IN BLOOD

Your people are drowning in blood and you're making poems!
And the January sun is ripening out of a smile,
shining on the cradle pillow of the first-born son:
there is a happiness not from here
and there is no tomorrow and no yesterday . . .
Hanging in the blue, she gives her tender caresses
to men blessed by God as well as to those who curse him.
In the amber of evening, in the red light of dawn,
she sleeps in the citrus branches
and casts their intricate splendors in gold leaf.

The sea—a glass of light, a glass of giants—
the sea in his green depths—
is he going to visit today his endless treasures,
nourish his eyes with the laughter of beryl and emerald,
comets of sapphire, heaps of turquoise,
light from the genesis of light, the embers of creation?
Whenever a cloud sails overhead on its vaporous wings,
he grows himself a skin of dark purple.

Come forward, range of mountains, angry and bluish . . .
I know a poem, a marvelous poem and only for me:
Oh golden and rose and spotted like the skin of leopards,
from before genesis, the mountains were here.
And their anger is frozen, anger still unavenged,
and their voices sleep under the crust of time.

Your stars are tiny suns, sown by a prodigal hand
on a velvet field of hyacinths whose lights fade out—
the night lays a wreath of such light on the head of the mountain
and a necklace round the throat of the Jordan.

The ancient mounds and pillars, your orphaned ruins—
there's no king's palace so full of song as they are.
And who will echo the song of every lump of earth,
every embattlement, that had so much bravery in them
they could not be killed?

The sea will open his mouth to scold the dry land,
a breaker will rise up toward the Ladder of Phoenicia,
the sun will conspire with light, guttering in the clouds,
and the seed of the stars will rot like wheat
in which gluttonous boars are rooting and grunting;
the desert will raise its voice in the lonely void,
and the mountains will convulse from head to foot
as in the day they unmade themselves into the plain of Sodom.
The garden bird will rest from its song,
if not for sorrow, if not for mourning, then . . .

And you, my country, my country, drunk with light, young,
your people are drowning in blood and you're making poems!

SAUL TCHERNICHOVSKY
Translated by Robert Mezey and Shula Starkman

EVE

I love Adam. He has a good heart,
his blood is generous, and he, like God,
is wise. But the serpent whispers things
that are so strange. They hurt—and they caress.

While Adam sleeps, Eden lies desolate;
its birds are silent and its grass is wet.
And then *he* kindles a bonfire in my heart,
calling from the underbrush, "Pick it! Pick it!"

How good to feel at dawn Adam's warm hand
caressing my body again, and in the silence
listen to the coursing of my blood.
But every bush that drinks the light by day
bends to a darkness. Eden's enchanted only
till night awakens the shadow among the leaves.

YAAKOV FICHMAN
Translated by Robert Friend

BLESSED ARE THEY THAT SOW

Blessed are they that sow and shall not reap
For they wander far.

Blessed are they that freely give all that they have,
The glory of their youth has made the sunlight richer
And they threw away their medals at the crossroads.

Blessed are they whose pride brims over their banks
And becomes white and humble
When the rainbow raises its arch in the clouds.

Blessed are they that know their hearts cry out in the wilderness.
Silence flowers on their lips.

Blessed, blessed are they, they shall be gathered to the heart of the
    world,
Warm in the coat of forgetfulness,
Eternal silence their offering
And their reward.

Avraham Ben Yitzhak
Translated by Robert Mezey

THE LONELY SAY

Day unto day bequeaths its trembling sun,
Night grieves for night.
Summer after summer is gathered in dead leaves,
And the world sings from its pain.

Tomorrow we shall die without a word
And when we depart, we shall stand at the closing gate,
And the heart, glad that God is bringing us close,
Will suddenly clench, fearing betrayal.

Day unto day lifts up a flaming sun,
And the nights pour out their stars.
On the lips of the lonely few, the song is finished:
By seven paths we part, and come back by one.

Avraham Ben Yitzhak
Translated by Robert Mezey

STOP PLAYING

Stop playing with words, you wastrels—
A true word is a wisdom tooth,
An agony tooth.
Steel screw driven into the flesh—
And there's no help, no end to this pain
Till it's pulled out
By the roots, twisted, naked,
Throbbing with blood.
And a man sighs gratefully when it's out at last,
Thrown down like a blood-sacrifice
On the altar of the world.
But for a long time he continues to lick
The deep hole
And he swallows the blood that oozes up.
Nothing will grow there again,
Forget it.
A wisdom tooth uprooted,
A word that escaped from the wise man's mouth—
They will not grow again,
Not in this world.

A man who has sought all his days—
O masters, do not mock "eternal love"
For a deep wound is woman,
Rib torn from the side,
Man flesh, animal flesh,
Stolen by God
When he had rummaged through creation
And could find nothing with which to finish his work . . .

And wounded man wanders all his days,
Searching for flesh, searching for bone
To close up that terrible mouth,
To stanch the blood—
And he stuffs his hollowness and pain
With whatever he comes across:
Flowering lilies,
Golden hair of flax,
Chunks of wood, loaves of stone,
Geese, doves, scratching rats . . .
But nothing fits.
"Not this!" he weeps to himself—
Even with his hand on the face of a lioness,
His heart weeps, "Not this!"
And so he goes stumbling on the path of love
Till he falls at a woman's feet—
Flesh of his flesh, bone of his bone!
But now the blood barely flows
And now the heart is empty and cold.
Only now does she fit,
The only one, the right one, O precious and clear one.
And the wound shuts like a grave.

ZALMAN SHNEOUR
Translated by Robert Mezey

REVOLT

Like a bird in the butcher's palm you flutter in my hand,
insolent pride.
I stop your mouth,
I press together the wings of your back,
and I laugh at you.
I've got you at last.
This is revenge for the flowers you plucked in their early bloom,
for your fences that cut off my path,
for the world whose rainbow colors you made dim.
Lie down in your corner of darkness till I return,
till I return from him.

RACHEL
Translated by Robert Friend

HIS WIFE

She turns and calls him by name
With the voice of every day.
How can I trust my voice
Not to give me away?

In the street, in the full light of day,
She walks by his side.
I in the dark of the night
Must hide.

Bright and serene on her hand
Is her ring of gold.
The iron fetters I wear
Are stronger, sevenfold.

RACHEL
Translated by Robert Friend

MY DEAD

They alone are left me; they alone still faithful,
for now death can do no more to them.

At the bend of the road, at the close of day,
they gather around me silently, and walk by my side.

This is a bond nothing can ever loosen.
What I have lost: what I possess forever.

RACHEL
Translated by Robert Mezey

IF NIGHT NEARS YOUR WINDOW

If night nears your window,
In nakedness come out to him.

He'll ripple softly, he'll darken
Round your still beauty,
Touching the tips of your breasts.

I'll stand, a lost traveller, with him,
And quietly we'll both feel desire.
Come to us, who are both darkling:

Your two eyes shall travel before
Us, to light
The way for me and my friend.

DAVID FOGEL
Translated by Dom Moraes

THE HOUR

The hour is very weary, as before sleep.
Like a foundling child, just in my white shirt,
I sit and write in space, as on a slate—
    No matter, no matter.

Should the black cat come to the pitcher and drink
The remnants of white milk and overturn the pitcher,
I will close my eyes to sleep and sleep forever—
    No matter, no matter.

URI ZVI GREENBERG
Translated by Robert Mezey and Ben Zion Gold

WITH MY GOD, THE SMITH

Like chapters of prophecy my days burn, in all the revelations,
And my body between them's a block of metal for smelting,
And over me stands my God, the Smith, who hits hard:
Each wound that Time has opened in me opens its mouth to him
And pours forth in a shower of sparks the intrinsic fire.

This is my just lot—until dusk on the road.
And when I return to throw my beaten block on a bed,
My mouth is an open wound,
And naked I speak with my God:
            You worked hard.
Now it is night; come, let us both rest.

Uri Zvi Greenberg
Translated by Robert Mezey and Ben Zion Gold

LIKE A WOMAN

Like a woman who knows that her body entices me,
God taunts me, Flee if you can! But I can't flee,
For when I turn away from him, angry and heartsick,
With a vow on my lips like a burning coal:
I will not see him again—

I can't do it,
>   I turn back
And knock on his door,
Tortured with longing

As though he had sent me a love letter.

Uri Zvi Greenberg
Translated by Robert Mezey and Ben Zion Gold

THE GREAT SAD ONE

The Almighty has dealt bitterly with me
That I did not believe in him until my punishment,
Till he welled up in my tears, from the midst of my wounds.
And behold, he also is very lonely,
And he also lacks someone to confess to,
In whose arms he might sob his unbearable misery—

And this God walks about, without a body, without blood,
And his grief is double the grief of flesh,
Flesh that can warm another body or a third,
That can sit and smoke a cigarette
And drink coffee and wine,
And sleep and dream until the sun—

For him it is impossible, for he is God.

Uri Zvi Greenberg
Translated by Robert Mezey and Ben Zion Gold

HOW IT IS

I hear the sound of affliction. They are weeping,
It seems—human beings, male and female.
Once I heard only the joy of those who were married
To the juice and sweetness of life.

There's no need to ask why they weep—it's clear enough.
If women are weeping, it's a sign of their defilement;
If men, what could it mean but the loss
Of great faiths as powerful as the earth?

Souls that go forth gaily on their wanderings,
Adorned with their colorful visions,
How wan they are, and shrunken, when they come back!

URI ZVI GREENBERG
Translated by Robert Mezey and Ben Zion Gold

THERE IS A BOX

There is a box and a coverlet, and a pair of black horses
Stepping forth heavily, in honor, of course, of the grief.
There is a spade, and a strong man, the digger,
White linen, and a girl who sews.

Adam is dust, the Rabbi must surely be rotting by now,
And what remains in writing—a doctrine of no death.
I speak of what feeds down there in the mire.
There is nothing in books, only a few words.

URI ZVI GREENBERG
Translated by Robert Mezey and Ben Zion Gold

THE VALLEY OF MEN

I have never been on the cloudy slopes of Olympus.
In the living man's valley I grew with the bread.
Like other men, I drank the sweet water there,
Waters where cattle drank, whose flesh I ate.

The Queen's train my forefathers did not carry, amongst the
    Gentiles.
The King did not call them, neither in sorrow nor in joy.
They were poor Jews, shining and singing,
Little more than the shepherd blows through his flute.

So I am pleased to carry myself from sorrow to sorrow,
As a shepherd his littlest sheep from pasture to pasture,
And he eats a few figs, to keep the breath in his body—

Red seamed are the ends of my days and nights.

URI ZVI GREENBERG
Translated by Robert Mezey and Ben Zion Gold

ON THE POLE

Some clouds are rainclouds—
On my head like a mist the mercy of sorrow transpires.
It is good to command the boat of all longings:
Stop and anchor.

For here is the Pole—and joy is native
To the place of childhood, garlanded with beauty.
It is good to descend, to rake in the remnants of honey
And the white milk—in the final place.

URI ZVI GREENBERG
Translated by Robert Mezey and Ben Zion Gold

TO THE MOUND OF
CORPSES IN THE SNOW

When they brought my father to the mound of corpses that was
in the snow in the strange field, the German officer screamed:
"Ausziehen!" And my father knew what he meant. My father,
like one who strips from himself the substance of this world, took
off his coat and his trousers, and drew off his shoes, as on the eve-
ning of the Fast of Av, and stood in his white underclothes and
his socks. What is more naked than such nakedness, under the
dome of the sky, on that day of the universe?

In all his days, he had not stood naked in his underclothes be-
neath the dome of the sky, wearing on his head his black skull-
cap, except at night before his bed, and in the bath-house in the
moment before he entered the water to be cleansed; for then only
did he take off his underclothes and his socks and remove his
skull-cap: he would not look at the nakedness of his body till the
water covered him. He entered as though to prostrate himself in
the depths.

But when the officer saw that my father was still standing in
his underclothes and his socks, and wearing on his head his black
skull-cap, the animal struck him with his cold weapon between
the shoulders and my father coughed and fell to the ground: as
before God. A prostration to the depths of his being from which
he did not rise. He gave a groan that was like the finishing of a
last prayer, after which there is no more prayer, only a clouded
sky, a heap of corpses, and a live officer, smoking in the snow-
covered plain. The snow on both sides of my saintly father's face
was melting, reddening, because of the blood that came out of his
mouth, from his burst lungs.

And when the officer saw that my father would not get to his feet, he worked the toe of his black jackboot into the belly of my holy father, and with a kick turned him over on his back. It looked as though the earth of the Gentiles itself had kicked in my father's face.

When night fell the stars glittered, the pile of corpses lay in the field, and snow came down out of the night with soft, cruel abundance. Such was God's will. The presence of a god was felt, but it belonged to the Gentiles. There is a God in the world, but there is no god of Israel.

Only the snow was witness: it came down, cruel, abundant.

Over that place my grandfather passed, the seraph, Rabbi Uri of Strelisk; whose steps made no sound there, the breath of whose nostrils left no ripple in the air. He opened his mouth and whispered,

"Rabbi Chaim, son of Rabbi Yitzhak Eliezer, grandson,
Body that was a harp for the prayers of Israel,
Mouth that gave comfort to the oppressed heart of
    Israel,
How does the snow cover you in the endless field of
    the Gentiles?
Where did your prayers go, my grandson,
Where did my prayers go,
To what abyss in the universe . . . ?"

From out of the heap of corpses crept my sister's little son, Shmuel, whom they fondly called Shmueltchy: he crept to the feet of our grandfather, the seraph, Rabbi Uri of Strelisk, and cried like a child, without opening his eyes, for he could not: with the palms of his small hands he beat on the shoes of our grandfather. Our grandfather bent down and kissed his forehead and said:

"O my baby, my martyred baby."

The child of my holy sister, the little boy Shmuel, whom they fondly called Shmueltchy, answered:

"O Zeyde, Zeyde, why didn't you come to us before
    with thousands of angels and seraphim?
O Zeyde, where is the god of the Jews?"

And the little boy was silent, lying at the feet of our grandfather, Rabbi Uri, who had delayed coming with his firebrands, who did not come to our house with thousands of angels and seraphim to defend us.

Rabbi Uri of Strelisk, the seraph, knelt frozen in the Gentile field, and the snow kept falling.

URI ZVI GREENBERG
Translated by A. C. Jacobs

WE WERE NOT LIKE DOGS

We were not like dogs among the Gentiles . . . they pity a dog,
They pet him, even kiss him with the Gentile mouth.
Like a fat baby, one of their very own,
They pamper him, always laughing and playing;
And when the dog dies, how bitterly the Gentiles mourn him!

We were not brought in the boxcars like lambs to the slaughter,
Rather, like leprous sheep,
Through all the beautiful landscapes of Europe,
They shipped us to Death.
They did not handle their sheep as they handled our bodies;
They did not yank out their teeth before they killed them;
Nor strip the wool from their bodies as they stripped our skin;
Nor shovel them into the fire to makes ashes of their life,
And scatter the ashes over streams and sewers.

Where are there other analogies to this,
This monstrous thing we suffered at their hands?
There *are* none—no other analogies! (All words are shadows of
    shadows)—
That is the horror: no other analogies!
No matter how brutal the torture a man may endure in a Christian
    country,
He who comes to compare will compare it thus:
He was tortured like a Jew.
Every fear, every anguish, every loneliness, every agony,
Every scream, every weeping in this world,
He who compares things will say:
This is the Jewish kind.

There is no retribution for what they did to us—
Its circumference is the world:

The culture of Christian kingdoms to its peak
Is covered with our blood,
And all their conscience, with our tears.

URI ZVI GREENBERG
Translated by Robert Mezey

DRESS ME, DEAR MOTHER

Dress me, dear mother, in splendor, a coat of many colors,
And at the break of dawn lead me to work.

My land lies wrapt in light as in a prayer shawl,
The houses stand forth like frontlets,
The asphalt roads we laid with our own hands
Branch out like the thongs of phylacteries.

Thus does a graceful city
Offer up morning prayers to the Creator.
And among the creators, your son Abraham,
Poet-roadbuilder in Israel.

And toward evening, father comes home from his labors
And whispers, as if praying, with quiet joy:
Abraham, my dear son,
All skin and bone and sinew,
Hallelujah!

Dress me, dear mother, in splendor, a coat of many colors,
And at the break of dawn, lead me
To work.

AVRAHAM SHLONSKY
Translated by Robert Mezey

[99

from JEZRAEL

Like hunchbacked old women the tents here hang out their
    tongues,
For the shoulder aches with the weight of the burden.
Man is flesh, and he labors here in holiness,
And bread comes from the earth.

Like a limping lamb here the world is carried
Under the armpit.
God's curls blow in the wind here,
Lightly touching every human cheek.

Who is great here, who is small
In the kingdom of work and very flesh?
The earth is unrolled here, the scroll of a new testament,
And we—we are twelve!

AVRAHAM SHLONSKY
Translated by Ruth Finer Mintz

SABBATH STARS

The Sabbath stars have climbed high, more peaceful than you
Who are sad today.
Your sadness is almost blasphemy—
Blowing out the careful candles Mother lit.

You, you who swore yourself into silence,
The essence of human speech,
Like honey, the privilege of a thousand roses,
Like a landscape where there is a pact of peace
Between wood and mountain and brook, to live as one,
Waging no wars, and yet to live alone—

Flow with your times and the children of your times,
Flow to your end as the river flows
To a known sea with a shore—

Where from wet sand the children knead new loaves,
And a seashell, knowing no words,
Still sighs in your ear the secret
Of low tide and high tide.

The Sabbath stars have climbed high, more peaceful than you.

AVRAHAM SHLONSKY
Translated by Dom Moraes

PARTING

And dawn shall trail after me to the shore,
Like a child, to play with shells:
Singing like a hope, shining like a tear,
Silent, the echo of what will befall.

On chill and sun he will inscribe his height
In a tall wide script: he shall not claim
Any remembrance of my form in flight,
My name, my humble other name,

My name which went singing for happiness,
For many griefs, and times I went astray.
With and above it, like a faltering promise
Stepped my great day.

A bit of it—like a scent, an echo—
I contained in the blue vase,
In the Chinese drawing made long ago,
Longing for its butterfly, its stalk of grass.

And a few books, not many, which looked out
At their moon leaving the river, on its way.
It taught a warm and festive solitude
And the sharp luster of the faraway.

When the parting suddenly flings wide forever
The unknown distance, in a little while,
I'll remember everything by name, by the quiver
Of their wise and bashful smile.

I shall put on my dead face with a silence free
Of joy and of pain forevermore,
And dawn will trail like a child after me
To play with shells on the shore.

YOCHEVED BAT-MIRIAM
Translated by Dom Moraes

DISTANCE SPILLS ITSELF

Distance spills itself and grows dazzling and blue,
Silver lights like scythes flashing in the meadow.
Who is it that seems to call and answer, who is it
That seduces my heart, full of longing like a wild bird?

Sadness, so much sadness, a night without daybreak,
Sadness like the river mist towering over the river.
Let me kiss the mezuzah nailed to my doorpost and be gone,
Like the poor man that entered and suddenly was gone.

I will meet a man who will not hear me approach,
The beasts of the field will be slow catching my scent,
The footpaths will drone like bells for my sake
And I'll whisper to my soul in pure solitude:

Oh let me walk alone, hearing voices
Crying "Holy holy holy," let me say "Amen,"
And suddenly I'll whisper, "Blessed be your name,"
Scorched by the mystery, by amazing grace . . .

Sadness, so much sadness. The distance stretches out,
Reminder of all that lies beyond the borders.
Not to be, to be gone—I pray for this
At the gates of infinity, like a fey child.

YOCHEVED BAT-MIRIAM
Translated by Robert Mezey and Shula Starkman

INCENSE

Night of sleeplessness,
night of no sleep.
I strap on my knapsack, containing nothing,
and go to discover a town that has no name.

A man is not a man,
a tower is not a tower,
but feels the height as though it pressed upon its spire;
but I from one window discover the whole world.

There I shall stand,
there, watching on high,
heart wholly still, body a whispering brand,
like a cloud of incense climbing towards the sky.

SHIN SHALOM
Translated by Robert Friend

NOT SO SIMPLE

It's not all so simple in the yards of houses;
Floor after floor, the windows stare into space.
On cracked pavements, on bare, faded walls,
Every passing hour has left its print.

It's not all so simple, how mirrors look at a room,
And there's something to read in the way the bookcase stands.
The heavy drapes, the carefully made bed
Are sinking down under the yoke of thought.

In every house there are many dark stairs.
Silent creatures come down them every morning
And go up every evening, and close their doors—
I pray for them . . .

SHIN SHALOM
Translated by Robert Mezey

THE OLIVE TREE

Summer has reigned
seventy years;
its mornings have poisoned with avenging light.
The olive tree alone,
my abandoned brother,
has not withdrawn in battle from their brightness.

How holy is its vow, for its black branches
bear neither star nor moon.
Only its poverty, like the Song of Songs, O Earth,
pierces the heart of your stones.

Perhaps from the eyes of its god, its lord,
one tear is granted, heavy and hot,
when like a bookkeeper, breathing anger,
he crouches lonely over your book.

When you wish your mountains to die
and herds bleat for rain and fodder,
it will stand watch on the wall, your solitary bridegroom,
and you will know your life is in its keeping.

And in the evening bleeding with the sunset
it will feel along your face— "Where are you?" . . .
In its twisted trunk, in the fire of its veins,
it keeps and preserves your tears.

When from the distance the red desert wind
springs violently forth,
it will withdraw
in terror,

for the mountain shall not fall, its heart shall not grow still
so long as one sapling
tears forth from its side.

NATAN ALTERMAN
Translated by Robert Friend

MOON

Also an old image has a moment of birth,
Sky without bird,
Strange and fortified.
On the moonlit night facing your window
Stands a city dipped in crickets' chirping.

And as you see the road still looking to the wayfarer
And the moon
On the cypress' spear,
You say: my God, are all these things still here?
Is it still permitted to whisper and ask how they are?

From its pools the water looks up at us.
The tree is tranquil
In its ruby earrings.
O God, it shall never be torn from me,
The sorrow of your great playthings.

NATAN ALTERMAN
Translated by Ruth Finer Mintz

SONG TO THE WIFE OF HIS YOUTH

My daughter, not all is vanity,
Not all is vanity.
I broke my promise to money,
I scattered my days in vain.
You alone I followed, my daughter,
As the neck follows the hangman.

You put on your kerchief, my daughter,
And you said: Look at me.
I vowed not to taste my bread
Till your greenness soured my teeth.
I vowed to look at you
Till my eyes were worn out with looking.

Then sickness struck, my daughter,
And poverty covered our faces.
And sickness I called "my house"
And poverty "my son."
We were poorer than dogs, my daughter.
Dogs ran away from us.

Then came iron, my daughter,
And beheaded me of you.
And nothing was left except
My ashes pursuing your shoes.
For iron is broken, my daughter,
But never my thirst for you.

My daughter, spirit is deathless,
But the body crumbles like clay.
Joy never came to my house
And the earth made me a cradle.
But the day my daughter rejoices,
My eyes will rejoice from the earth.

The day of joy is coming,
There is still a hand and a rope.
You will enter the earth of our promise,
They will lower you with ropes.
Not all is vanity, my daughter,
Not all is vanity.

NATAN ALTERMAN
Translated by Robert Mezey and Shula Starkman

BEYOND MELODY

With a violin in the alley grandfather and son disappeared.
Again the night was closed. Speak to me, please speak!
I who grew up with all your stones,
I knew—they too would break, like confessions.

Stones like tears in the lashes of the world.
How should I set out to wipe them with a silken cloth?
Over the last song that trembles around them,
Silence glides like an eagle.

Sometimes from the night we open astonished eyes
And slowly we smile, out of our wisdom and folly.
Mother's greyness looks at our lives,
The silence of rooms where there is no child.

And we shall go out to pale roads we abandoned—
They stand erect with a song and a cloud,
They will go tall, tenderly in their strength,
They will go rocking us in their bosom—

Go and tell them
The well is filled,
The forest is burning in its sovereign mantle.
But deaf and alone,
Ashamed and tiny,
Our pain is tilling its field.

For it has no messiah and it has no flags.
Silences dressed in mourning guard its cradles.
It lives in solitude, like its older brothers,
The end, the heart, and the autumn.

It shines with the light of a mother's forgiveness,
In the shy stillness of wisdom and folly—
On the lips of thresholds thirsty and wide
Its smile is stoned at our feet.

NATAN ALTERMAN
Translated by Robert Mezey and Shula Starkman

THE SILVER TRAY

A state is not handed to a people on a silver tray.
—Chaim Weizmann

. . . And the country is quiet. The red eye of heaven
blinks slowly, growing dark
on the smoking borders.
And the nation stands—heart torn but breathing—
to receive the miracle
that is like nothing else.

She readies herself for the ceremony. She rises
facing the moon and stands, before dawn,
wrapt in festival and terror.
—Then, from the darkness, a girl and a boy
will come forth
and slowly, slowly, walk towards their people.

Dressed in workclothes, wearing web belts and heavy boots,
they are climbing the path,
keeping silence.
They never changed clothes
or washed away the footprints
of the day of labor and the endless night of gunfire.

Infinitely weary, having taken vows not to rest,
and dripping with the dew of Hebrew youth—
quietly the two of them draw near
and stand motionless.
And there is no way of telling
whether or not there are bullets in their flesh.

Then the nation, rinsed by tears and by magic,
will ask: Who are you? And the two, silent till now,
will speak: We are the silver tray
on which the Jewish homeland is handed to you.

So they say. And collapse at her feet, wrapt in shadow.
And the rest will be told in the books of the chronicles
             of Israel.

NATAN ALTERMAN
Translated by Robert Mezey and Shula Starkman

OF BLOOM

I

The flowering castor, abruptly at night grown dense,
Crimson and warm in leaves that are velvety black.
A line of trees that lean on a barbed-wire fence.

The flocks that rested until their limbs were slack
Lag down from the field to the fold. And overhead
The restless blue shakes a white cloud off its back.

These will fade, as lights in the water fade,
But endure in the wild smell of the field and wood.
At sundown the young grass is soft and red

Almost as if it grew from my silent blood.

2

An aged woman, sunburned, with blue eyes,
Crowned by her suffering and her white hair.
The pail brims silver. From the barndoors rise

Rich vaporous smells that spread across the air.
There is a law of life in her hands milking,
For quiet seamen hold a rope like her.

Here the submissive cows, the unclouded morning.
A woman above flowing white. An ordinary day.
The cloudy secret of a primeval thing,

And the sorceress crouched above her mystery.

LEAH GOLDBERG
Translated by Dom Moraes

SONG OF THE STRANGE WOMAN

1

I am green and replete like a song that has blown through the
    grass,
I am deep and soft as a bird-nest,
I come from yesterday,
from the forest that taught me to breathe,
from the well where I drank of the light,
from the exhausted lovers embraced and sleeping in the grass.

I am from there,
from the village of the small winds,
from skies that weave low clouds with bluish smoke.

I hear your voices still,
blue as your smoke, and dim.
I come from the village of clattering wooden spoons.
I am from there.

    2

Windmill, windmill,
on what shore did the gulls cry
the name of my dead land?
Windmill, windmill.

On what street did they walk
who did not turn their heads,
the kingdom of the sunset on their backs?
And the wings drummed in the wind.

Where?
Is the garden there, crimson
with autumn, burying shadows,
hiding the twilights under the leaves,
making way, making way for the wind?

And the wind, and the gull, did they cry
the name of my dead land?
Windmill, windmill!

    3

Land of low clouds, I belong to you.
I carry in my heart your every drop of rain.
On stumbling feet, without an angel to lean on, I travel towards
    you,
bringing mushrooms of your forest to the kingdom of heaven.

In the kingdom of heaven, they still remember your feast day.
A gay harmonica is playing the song of the dead.
And a star entangled in the arms of the wind
is turning, turning—
and I have grown old, grown gray, and who will dance with me?

Nevertheless, for the gate is open there,
I shall be at the festival:
I shall take off my shoes and sit down in the shade.
Slowly my face will float on a lazy stream,
my face lit up by the rivers
of your remembered shores.
Windmill, windmill!

LEAH GOLDBERG
Translated by Robert Friend

BIRTH

The rain is over.

Yet from branches and eaves
It whispers in my ears
And covers my face
With a bluish bridal veil.

Good for you, God,
The child is caught in your net.
Now I shall bring leaf close to leaf,
Now I shall watch how leaf covers leaf

And the drops run together,
And I'll summon to my wedding
The swallows out of the sky.
And crown my windows with flower pots.

Good for you, God,
The child is caught in your net.
I open my eyes—
My land is very wide,
Everything a field of tangled
Green buds.

O God, how embraced we have been!

AMIR GILBOA
Translated by Robert Mezey and Shula Starkman

THE CIRCLE OF WEEPING

I heard the weeping of the newly born in its mother's bosom
And as I returned, the weeping of the mother over her young.
And I did not stop or try to speak
And I did not ask who did her wrong
For this was the closed circle of weeping—
                            the fixed song
That circles between the mother and her young.

AMIR GILBOA
Translated by Ruth Finer Mintz

BLUE AND RED POEM

You walked as if in snow. And you walked in snow.
Bears rose up against you! Papa Bear. Mama Bear. Baby Bear.
You ran as hard as you could. You thought you were falling,
And the terror of thousands of years was in your eyes.

And now, here you are. Years have passed.
The beautiful bears are gone. Will they ever come back?
Tonight in our garden, branches broke
And the broken places are still dripping blood and tears.

So that's how it is. We are young.
Yet, in our memory, thousands of years old.
See, all the images drawn up outside your window
In a single line. Yet none is far, none is near.

AMIR GILBOA
Translated by Robert Mezey and Shula Starkman

BLIND ANGEL

Of life and its ceasing to be, with changes of sea wind
    Dawn tide on the cliffs
    Sundown poem beating
        On the headlands of night.

As the shining wave breaks on the current, sunlight breaks into
           pieces.
    A cloud goes by in the image of a blind angel.
    The moon embalms dead darkness. A blind snake at the
        threshold.

Until the blue of prayer is kindled in the canopy of desire
    Like the stillness of lakes in the heatwaves before dusk.

Rest, sea, in the twilight gathering between day and night—
    Elegy of the shore fluttering requiem for illusions.
    Heart's scaffold in its loneliness. Inconsolable song,
        Whistling of the border wind.

Like the ocean floor
    Midnight collects anguish of many daggers
Unsheathed from the soul's bitterness in the blaze of noon.
On a bed of quicksand night thickens,
        Stripped bare of dreams, and conspiring.

DAVID ROKEAH
Translated by Robert Mezey and Shula Starkman

THE WALL

The tottering wall has underground thoughts
and moss lining the cracks.
Tomorrow or the next day—a border flare-up
a parchment scroll
in an unearthed jar.

While there is still time, the sentries will sing for summer
that flutters in dug-outs like the wind in hedges.
They shut the night, and nights that will follow it
in barbed-wire cages, in the bereavement of lapsed time,
in an instant of hatred
stretched to a generation. They mutter
Amen to a jackal
that violates the border. Thorns
flowering as a last hope for no-man's land.

DAVID ROKEAH
Translated by Bernard Lewis

ODYSSEUS

And returning at last to his birthplace he found the ocean
and various fish and seaweed gliding on the slow waves.
A sun weakening on the hem of the sky.

Error forever recurs, thought Odysseus, sick at heart,
as he made his way to the cross-roads near the city
to look for a road to a birthplace that was not water.

A wanderer like a man exhausted by dreams and longings,
among people who spoke some other Greek—
the words he had carried for provisions had meanwhile gone bad.

For a moment he imagined he had slept a long time
and come back to people who were not surprised to see him,
people whose eyes regarded him blankly.

He questioned them with his hands and they tried to understand,
from a distance.
The crimson was darkening, fading, in the hem of that sky.

At last they took hold of the children who had gathered around
      him
and led them away.
And light after light glowed yellow in house after house.

The dew came and touched him on the forehead.
Came wind and kissed him on the lips.
Came water and washed his feet, like the old nurse,
and did not notice the scar
and went running on down the slope, as water does.

CHAIM GURI
Translated by Robert Mezey and Shula Starkman

PICTURES OF THE JEWS

My quiet prison guards, much tried. My lovers.
Their glances stroke my face until the end.
I am there.
Dungeon. Stones, iron and twilight.
They do not come to me now by inheritance.

I see them:
Half of them alive and half of them dead,
Free men.
Easy smugglers, of subtle understanding,
Who know by heart the approaches to the sky
And it is there they wander, as to a familiar country.
And their faces are like the faces of weary sages.

They return, in hours of weak-mindedness, to strange earth,
To look about and to meditate.
They return like renters.
After a short time their faces are in blood.

And they wander, wander and scatter in the wind,
Wind that erases footprints,
Wind that carries the smell of the dead,
Like an agent traveling and weary, black and white,
Who sells wind and trembling.

And his beard grows on the way,
And his house is far away, high up, beyond the silence.

They come to me,
Their footstep close to silence
And fearful like mortal danger. They come here.
Invade me, leaving a sad victory,
And retreat in me silently to the royal city, ancient and far.

They come to me, out of the sickness.
From beyond forests and lands and water.
Their faces return from the tear that salted the sea.

Their faces are the smile of the sages,
Above stones and metal and dark pitch
I dream them.

The inhabitants of the city sense them suddenly:
Thieves on ladders to the clouds.
When they shoot at them,
Half their outcry falls with them.
Half rises to the sky, which is used to it,
To be received,
To become the song of the angels.

And tonight they return to attack me with prolonged attacks,
Footprints in blood, blood everywhere.

I do not move now.
I carry on, as if enchanted, their movements,
And they go on and are murdered within me like a father.
And they are alone.
And only God is with them.

CHAIM GURI
Translated by Ruth Finer Mintz

PIYYUT FOR ROSH HASHANA

For this is not the road against which stand enemy lines, or for-
eign languages,
Or muteness.
Neither I nor my voice is tied by the conditions set on these dis-
tances.
I walk and I am not murdered.
I come at last to the house. I stop. I knock at the door.

All men who forgive say, What has been has been. I repeat it.
All women who forgive stand on the porches sooner or later.
There is a window which is not black. There is a letter which is
not lost on the way.
And if it did not arrive yesterday, it will surely arrive tomorrow.

All the cities are open tonight. None is besieged or embalmed.
Guests will arrive tonight and I am one of them.
In all the windows, branches of regret are opening one after an-
other.
Many words come up in pilgrimage from lands of silence and
death.

The curtains billow and the doors move on their hinges.

CHAIM GURI
Translated by Ruth Finer Mintz

THOSE WHO GO, NOT TO RETURN

It's not the dead that shall praise you today, O Lord!
The torn bodies drip, one by one.
And even if it is like that for us—more or less—
They are the ones who go, not to return.

Their names are covered with darkness now, Lord God.
One by one they went, but they did not arrive.
The murdered child returned to his dust,
His mouth torn open by a forest of roots.

Also, our memory is bad. We cannot foretell.
Those who have gone—prayers will not bring them back.
What more can we do to you that we have not done?
What more, little brother, drowned in lies?

Not forever will your girl be red with weeping
And not forever will she cast down her eyes.
In your native village the bells moan
As if you had not gone and had not come back.

And the soul of man? Does she endure forever?
Who says so, whether in kindness or anger?
Better the living dog than the dead lion,
For life is given us once, and never again.

BENJAMIN GALAI
Translated by Robert Mezey and Shula Starkman

HANDFULS OF WIND

All that I have—
Handfuls of wind,
A gift for the kingdom of birds.

All the silences—
A throatful of small silences,
A present
For the stone and the doe.

All the illumination—
Flask of illumination,
For the sea of rising dawn
An offering.

With all one's heart
With all one's might
As both innocent and guilty.

And my eyes shall not see
The ocean overflowing
Its banks . . .

YEHIEL MAR
Translated by Ruth Finer Mintz

AS FOR THE WORLD

As for the world,
I am always like one of Socrates' disciples,
Walking by his side,
Hearing his opinions and histories;
It remains for me to say:
Yes. Yes, it is like that.
You are right again,
Indeed your words are true.

As for my life,
I am always like Venice:
Whatever is mere streets in others
Within me is a dark streaming love.

As for the cry, as for the silence,
I am always a shofar:
All year long hoarding its one blast
For the Terrible Days.

As for action,
I am always like Cain:
Nomad
In the face of the act, which I will not do,
Or, having done,
Will make it irredeemable

As for the palm of your hand,
As for the signals of my heart
And the plans of my flesh,
As for the writing on the wall,
I am always ignorant;

I can neither read nor write
And my head is like the
Heads of those senseless weeds,

Knowing only the rustle and drift
Of the wind
When a fate passes through me
To some other place.

YEHUDA AMICHAI
Translated by Assia Gutmann

ON MY BIRTHDAY

Thirty-two times I went forth to my life.
Each time it pained my mother less,
Pained others less
And me more.

Thirty-two times I put on the world
And still it does not fit me.
It burdens me,
Unlike my overcoat whose shape now
Is the shape of my body, comfortable
And growing worn.

Thirty-two times I went over the account
Without finding the error.
I began the story
And was not allowed to finish it.

Thirty-two years I carried with me my father's qualities
And most of them I dropped by the roadside
To ease the burden.
Grass in my mouth. I wonder,
And the beam I am unable to remove from my eyes
Begins to flower with the trees in springtime.

My deeds grow fewer,
Progressively fewer,
But commentaries on them have increased:
Just as the Talmud grows difficult
Concentrated on a page,
And footnotes and glosses on footnotes
Enclose it on every side.

And now for the thirty-second time
After the thirty-second year
I am still a parable
With no chance of a moral.
I stand without camouflage before enemy eyes,
With obsolete maps in my hands,
With growing opposition and surrounded by towers,
Alone without recommendations
In a great wilderness.

YEHUDA AMICHAI
Translated by Ruth Finer Mintz

LEAVES WITHOUT TREES

Leaves without trees
Have to wander.
Blood without a body
Will not return again to the body,
It will cake on all the roads,
And all the words must be weaned
From the mouth
To find out new ones.
The earth must recover
From its history
And the stones have to sleep,
Even the one
Which toppled Goliath must sleep in the darkness.

And I
Like a garage
Converted into a synagogue,
And again abandoned.

And I
Like a surveyor
With black and white sticks
Must drive my sharpened hopes
Deep into the barren plain
Before me.

YEHUDA AMICHAI
Translated by Robert Mezey and Shula Starkman

MAYOR

It's sad
To be the Mayor of Jerusalem.
It is terrible.
How can any man be the mayor of a city like that?

What can he do with her?
He will build, and build, and build.

And at night
The stones of the hills round about
Will crawl down
Towards the stone houses,
Like wolves coming
To howl at the dogs
Who have become men's slaves.

YEHUDA AMICHAI
Translated by Assia Gutmann

NATIONAL THOUGHTS

You: trapped in the homeland of the Chosen People.
On your head a cossack's fur hat,
Child of their pogroms.
"After these words." Always.
Or, for instance, your face: slanting eyes,
Pogrom Year eyes. Your cheekbones, high,
Hetman's cheekbones, Hetman the rabble king.
Hassid dancing, dutiful, you, naked on a rock in the early
    evening by the canopies of water at Ein Geddi
With eyes closed and your body open like hair.

After these words, "Always."
Every day I know the miracle of
Jesus walking upon the waters,
I walk through my life without drowning.

To speak, now, in this tired language
Torn from its sleep in the Bible—
Blinded, it lurches from mouth to mouth—
The language which described God and the Miracles,
Says:
Motor car, bomb, God.

The squared letters wanted to stay closed,
Every letter a locked house,
To stay and to sleep in it forever.

YEHUDA AMICHAI
Translated by Assia Gutmann

THEY CALL ME

Taxis below
And angels above
Are impatient.
At one and the same time
They call me
With a terrible voice.

I'm coming, I am
Coming,
I'm coming down,
I'm coming up!

YEHUDA AMICHAI
Translated by Assia Gutmann

TO MY MOTHER

1

Like an old windmill,
Two hands always raised
To howl at the sky
And two lowered
To make sandwiches.

Her eyes are clean and glitter
Like the Passover eve.

2

At night she will put
All the letters
And the photographs
Side by side.

So she can measure
The length of God's finger.

3

I want to walk in the deep
Wadis between her sobs,
I want to stand in the terrible heat
Of her silence.

I want to lean on the
Rough trunks
Of her pain.

4

She laid me
As Hagar laid Ishmael
Under one of the bushes.

So that she won't have to be at my death
In the war,
Under one of the bushes
In one of the wars.

Y EHUDA A MICHAI
Translated by Assia Gutmann

I WAS THE MOON

My child is very sad.

Whatever I teach him—
Geography of love,
Strange languages that can't be heard
Because of the distance—
My child rocks his little bed towards me in the night.
What am I?
More than forgetting.
The very language of forgotten.
And until he understands what I did
I am as good as dead.

What are you doing with our quiet child?
You cover him with a blanket
Like heaven, layers of clouds—
I could be the moon.

What are you doing with your sad fingers?
You dress them with gloves
And go out.

I was the moon.

Y EHUDA A MICHAI
Translated by Assia Gutmann

IN THE MIDDLE OF THIS CENTURY

In the middle of this century we turned to each other
With half faces and full eyes
Like an ancient Egyptian picture
And for a short while.

I stroked your hair
In the opposite direction to your journey.
We called to each other,
Like calling out the names of towns
Where nobody stops
Along the route.

Lovely is the world rising early to evil,
Lovely is the world falling asleep to sin and pity,
In the mingling of ourselves, you and I,
Lovely is the world.

The earth drinks men and their loves
Like wine,
To forget.
And it can't.
And like the contours of the Judean hills,
We shall never find peace.

In the middle of this century we turned to each other,
I saw your body, throwing shade, waiting for me,
The leather straps for a long journey
Already tightening across my chest.
I spoke in praise of your mortal hips,
You spoke in praise of my passing face.

I stroked your hair in the direction of your journey,
I touched your flesh, prophet of your end,
I touched your hand, which has never slept,
I touched your mouth, which may yet sing.

Dust from the desert covered the table
At which we did not eat.
But with my finger I wrote on it
The letters of your name.

YEHUDA AMICHAI
Translated by Assia Gutmann

THE PLACE WHERE I HAVE NOT BEEN

The place where I have not been
I never shall be.
The place where I have been
Is as though I have never been there. People stray
Far from the places where they were born
And far from the words which were spoken
As if by their mouths
And still wide of the promise
Which they were promised.

And they eat standing and die sitting
And lying down they remember.
And what I shall never in the world return to
And look at, I am to love forever.
Only a stranger will return to my place. But I will set down
All these things once more, as Moses did,

After he smashed the first tablets.

Yehuda Amichai
Translated by Assia Gutmann

from SPANISH MUSIC IN WINTER

Olé. All yea. All no. No. He who is getting old and slow
will rush away in a swift airplane. The snow
has already covered the scene of disaster. A long arm
spread black beads on it with
a masterful gesture. We have
nothing to lose. Urgency
is dominating us. Sex
is submitting to a foreign rhythm. A strip of fire
is consuming, kangaroo-like, jungle after jungle, lad after lad,
lady after lad. Was it good, was it bad?
Was it exactly like mamma said?
Europe is aging. All its hope
lies in the Pelviterranean Basin, the new course, the new
intercourse, the long unyielding summer, the small
dark Italians conquering America in narrow beds after
a backbreaking workday. How,
how was it, Marcello? How the hell has he
picked up that chassis? Now
let us return at long last to the point. It's cold. Summer
sends postcards too seldom. It has nothing
to report. It wishes to export
itself to another planet while
there's still time. The bull is frightened,
the bull is pushing the earth backwards, he
belongs to the avant-garde. Something
will happen this very evening, precisely
under the strict discipline of
the castanets. How could we have
so long overlooked
the castanets?

DAVID AVIDAN
Translated by David Avidan

THE STAIRCASE

Six seven minutes after death
everything will hang on the circumstances.
The hanged man and the circumstances
will hang on the circumstances only six
seven minutes. Who
will come?
Whoever wishes
to
will come,
whoever wishes
too
late.
Six seven minutes after death
nothing will fly nothing will flow nothing
will come. Siegfried Selinger
will come, A-1 qualified
locksmith from Strassburg member
of the Palestine Pioneer Union third
floor results guaranteed fourth
floor angina pectoris six
seven minutes after death six
seven minutes after Selinger.

DAVID AVIDAN
Translated by David Avidan

THE CONDITION

First I'll sing. Later, perhaps, I'll speak.
I'll repeat the words

Like someone memorizing his face at morning.
I'll return to my silences

The way the moon wanes.
In public I'll hoist the black fowl of sorrow

Like a boy drawing his sword on Purim.
I'll court your closed hands

Like a lantern that is endlessly blackening.
So, I'll return, keep silence, weep,

And I'll sing. First I'll sing. I'll wrap the words
In paper bags, like pomegranates.

Later, perhaps, we'll speak.

T. CARMI
Translated by Peter Everwine and Shula Starkman

SNOW IN JERUSALEM

If not today
    In the glitter and the searing of this white,
When shall we sense the hearts of birds, soft flood
Throbbing awake, as they alight
In the branchy landscape of our blood:

If not today
    Hearing the peaks, their white flesh veiled above,
When shall we rise, open of hand and face—
With the shoot of their love
At the crossing of the ways:

If not today
    Facing the olive shawled in what is strange,
When, piercing the cave of the heart, shall we hear the cry
Echoed, the word in change,
Shed from our sky:

If not today
    Hearing a man fearful of his own roof,
When shall we go, purer than this light here
To sing with him the psalm, the proof
Of the death of fear:

To sing with him,
    O victor, blood true and awake,
That he should not bow his head
At the terrible daybreak.

T. CARMI
Translated by Dom Moraes

from QUATRAINS

GENTLEMAN TO LADY

Breasts small as shells from the sea.
If they cupped my ears, as I wish,
I would hear quivering within me
Lovely nocturnal fish.

SHELL TO GENTLEMAN

It's very difficult for two shells to speak
Freely together. Each listens to its own sea call.
It remains for the pearl-diver or the peddler of the antique
To say with firmness: "Same sea, after all."

T. CARMI
Translated by Dom Moraes

from THE BRASS SERPENT

THE MAN SPEAKS

I know the serpent has unsheathed himself
Like a sword, and dressed in light like the Spring,
I know the seraph has spread like the dazzle of the sun
A burning wing.
How can I raise my human eyes to him?

I know that whoever dares to raise his eyes
He will save.
I know that now he is crying aloud,
O burnished and cold, O kingdom of sleep and the wave—
How can I not be ashamed to look at him nude?

I know further that my fingers are scaly,
Reptilian and old. I know that the rod
Of the reeking serpent once flowered within the wall
Of the tabernacle of God.
What would I do with my hands if they flowered and dew fell?

I know that the people see the mountain and the holy voices.
But already they buy and sell the cast skins
Of the serpent. I know that the plague will only
Come to the people again.
Am I strong enough to be like a leper, and lonely?

I look. I look. My eyes,
Nervous reptilian heads, draw in
And out, grubbing for darkness from above.
I look, and it is the earth at which I am looking.
I feel my blood flowing.

MIRIAM

And Moses made a serpent of brass

Miriam, Miriam, dancer and sister
To the sea and the high tide of the drum
By my side like a living well
Rise, rise.
Teach me to bless the portent,
The morning light of the gazelle,
And the terror of my eyes.

And put it upon a pole, and it came to pass

Miriam, Miriam, prophetess and sister
To murder, flower, snake,
Teach me to conceal what I can,

To reveal myself, a striking seraph, and to raise
My hands to the tabernacle of the whitening snow
Like one who prays.

That if a serpent had bitten any man

Miriam, Miriam, leper and sister
To spittle, to shame,
Teach me to be
Like one dead, outside the camp.
Teach me to speak truthfully.
Teach me to raise my eyes:

When he beheld the serpent of brass, he lived.

T. CARMI
Translated by Dom Moraes

AT THE SCORPIONS' ASCENT

Suddenly,
into my eyes, exploded God.
Thoughtless,
indifferent to glory of dreams, before me broke—
    cliff-mountains on the road to Araba Valley.

Wildness of open spaces,
endlessness of the stone laughing terrors, legend of the pit,
exploded the Lord God of the desert:
making clamorous the heights of Edom's mountains. God of
    a strange land, unguessable landscape,
    waste land of dreaming metal;

no wind—but ether flowing,
no sun—but electric myriads.
A curtain of tears enveloped me from God
    as from a heavy wind.
      Or from a thundering sun
      or from the lightning of the spirit being broken.

I thought nothing. I only breathed molten lead.
And I heard the men, the soldiers that were with me
    crying voicelessly,
    hammered dumb.
And I sat on the cold steel
    cast by human hands,
and I grasped the cold steel
    cast by human hands that man might kill himself,
    without entering into the secret knowledge of Eternity.
Rejected, heavy with wonders, open to the madness of greatness,
God was before me. As he is, adorned with ugliness according to
      his will.
    Eternal,—
    knowing no seers!
Free to ruin the multitudes of his glory, and the men
    powerless to bear this burden will not die,
      but will not be so foolish as to sacrifice to him their petti-
      nesses and prayers.
He alone and his mountains,
desert of the planetary metal.

At the Scorpions' Ascent he set down lightning and its magic to
      be a road,
At the Scorpions' Ascent he exploded into my eyes.
    And I grasped the cold steel.
And perhaps I was not I, but my enemy, Ishmael or Egypt,

but I was a man in the world, and my hand grasped death and
       cold steel,
    and I was an outcast, aspiring to pettiness.
And from before me Eternity stormed!

Tears wrapped my eyes, for I was an outcast.
And my eyes were too small to bear the land of the scorpions,
and I wept unconsoled:

Lord God,
why did you create me a man, while my heart is dying to be
       a desert, to be mountains, to be wind!
    And my eyes—to be sky, and sun!
And you placed in my hands cold steel to kill your little creatures,
and I, my stature is but a few cubits and I go to kill locusts like
       me,
    whose stature is but a few cubits,
    while my spirit is dashed to pieces to be Eternity!
And to you, my God, there is no end of light-years, Being of All!

At the Scorpions' Ascent on the road to Araba Valley, opposite
       Edom,
I saw my nothingness, till I ceased my weeping.

Lord my God.
Bring silence down on my spirit.
Shut my heart from before you with gates of stone or Topheth.
Remove your world from my eyes, bring night on the earth;
    Lord my God, Lord my God, bring night!

OMER HILLEL
Translated by Sholom J. Kahn

I SAW

I saw a white bird disappear in the black night
and I knew it wouldn't be long for the light
of my eyes in that same night.

I saw a cloud as small as a man's hand
and I knew, though the first ripples widen in the pond,
that I haven't been able to make anyone understand.

I saw a leaf that fell, a leaf is falling.
Time is short. I am not complaining.

NATAN SACH
Translated by Robert Mezey

Index of Titles

All Things Come Alike to All, 32
Alone, 73
Apple, The, 62
Apple for Isaac, An, 58
Arise, My Love, 35
As for the World, 127
At the Scorpions' Ascent, 145

Basket of Summer Fruit, The, 49
Behold, Thou Art Fair, My Love, 37
Beyond Melody, 110
Birth, 116
Blessed Are They That Sow, 83
Blind Angel, 119
Blue and Red Poem, 118
Born Without a Star, 64
Brass Serpent, *from* The, 143
By the Rivers of Babylon, 30

Circle of Weeping, The, 117
Complaint to God, The, 18
Condition, The, 141
Cups Without Wine, 63

David's Lamentation, 17
Denunciation of the Princes and Prophets, A, 51
Distance Spills Itself, 104
Dress Me, Dear Mother, 99

Eve, 82

Fire of Love, The, 40
From the Prophecy Against Egypt, 41

Grave, The, 79
Graves, 59
Great Sad One, The, 91

Handfuls of Wind, 126
His Answer to the Critics, 57
His Wife, 88
Hour, The, 89
How Beautiful Are Thy Feet with Shoes, 38
How It Is, 92

I Have a Garment, 65
I Saw, 148
I Was the Moon, 134

I Will Extol Thee, O Lord, 20
If Night Nears Your Window, 89
In the Middle of This Century, 136
In the Morning I Look for You, 58
Incense, 105
Invitation, The, 44

Jerusalem, 62
Jezrael, *from*, 100
Judgment and Sunrise, 53

Leaves Without Trees, 130
Like a Woman, 90
Lonely Say, The, 84
Lord Hath Done Great Things for Us, The, 28
Lord, Thou Hast Been Our Dwelling Place, 23

Man Is Nothing But, 76
Mayor, 131
Meditation on Providence, A, 25
Moon, 108
Mount Avarim, 60
My Dead, 88
My Heart Is in the East, 61
My Stars, 64

National Thoughts, 131
Not So Simple, 106

O Lord, Save We Beseech Thee, 66

O Thou Seer, Go, Flee Thee Away, 72
Odysseus, 121
Of Bloom, 113
Olive Tree, The, 107
On My Birthday, 128
On Slaughter, 74
On the Gifts of God, 29
On the Pole, 94

Parting, 102
Pictures of the Jews, 122
Piyyut for Rosh Hashana, 124
Place Where I Have Not Been, The, 138
Prayer to Be Delivered from Liars and Warmongers, A, 27
Prayer to Be Restored to the Sanctuary, A, 22
Prophecies Against Moab, Judah, and Israel, The, 48
Psalms, 20–30

Quatrains, *from*, 143

Rejoice Not, O Israel, for Joy, 46
Remember Now Thy Creator, 34
Revolt, 87

Sabbath Stars, 101
Secret Kept, A, 63
Silver Tray, The, 112
Snow in Jerusalem, 142
Song of Solomon, The (Excerpts), 35–40

Song of Thanksgiving, A, 28
Song of the Strange Woman, 114
Song to the Wife of His Youth, 109
Spanish Music in Winter, *from*, 139
Staircase, The, 140
Stop Playing, 85

There Is a Box, 92
They Call Me, 132
Those Who Go, Not to Return, 125
To Moses ibn Ezra, in Christian Spain, 60
To My Mother, 133

To the Mound of Corpses in the Snow, 95
Twilight Piece, 71

Valley of Men, The, 93

Wall, The, 120
War, 57
We Were Not Like Dogs, 98
With My God, the Smith, 90
Writing of Hezekiah King of Judah, When He Had Been Sick, And Was Recovered of His Sickness, The, 43

Your People Are Drowning in Blood, 80

Index of First Lines

A girl brought me into the house of love, 63
All that I have, 126
Also an old image has a moment of birth, 108
And dawn shall trail after me to the shore, 102
And I said, Hear, I pray you, O heads of Jacob, 51
And returning at last to his birthplace he found the ocean, 121
. . . And the country is quiet. The red eye of heaven, 112
And where are the graves, so many graves, 59
As for the world, 127

Beautiful heights, city of a great King, 62
Behold, thou art fair, my love, 37
Bless the Lord, O my soul, 25
Blessed are they that sow and shall not reap, 83
Breasts small as shells from the sea, 143

By the rivers of Babylon, there we sat down, 30

Cups without wine are low things, 63

Day unto day bequeaths its trembling sun, 84
Distance spills itself and grows dazzling and blue, 104
Dress me, dear mother, in splendor, a coat of many colors, 99

Except the Lord build the house, 29

First I'll sing. Later, perhaps, I'll speak, 141
Flee thee away? A man like myself doesn't flee, 72
For all this I considered in my heart, 32
For, behold, the day cometh, 53
For this is not the road against which stand enemy lines, 124

Heaven, ask pity for me, 74
Ho, every one that thirsteth, come ye to the waters, 44
How, after you, can I find rest, 60
How amiable are thy tabernacles, O Lord of hosts, 22
How beautiful are thy feet with shoes, 38

I am green and replete like a song that has blown through the grass, 114
I am the rose of Sharon, and the lily of the valleys, 35
I come in the morn, 64
I have a garment which is like a sieve, 65
I have never been on the cloudy slopes of Olympus, 93
I hear the sound of affliction. They are weeping, 92
I heard the weeping of the newly born in its mother's bosom, 117
I know the serpent has unsheathed himself, 143
I love Adam. He has a good heart, 82
I said in the cutting off of my days, 43
I saw a white bird disappear in the black night, 148
I will extol thee, O Lord, for thou hast lifted me up, 20
If it had not been the Lord who was on our side, 28

If night nears your window, 89
If not today, 142
In my distress I cried unto the Lord, 27
In the middle of this century we turned to each other, 136
In the morning I look for you, 58
Is there not an appointed time to man upon earth, 18
It's not all as simple in the yards of houses, 106
It's not the dead that shall praise you today, O Lord!, 125
It's sad, 131

Leaves without trees, 130
Like a bird in the butcher's palm you flutter in my hand, 87
Like a girl who knows that her body has brought me to begging, 90
Like an old windmill, 133
Like chapters of prophecy my days burn, in all the revelations, 90
Like hunchbacked old women the tents here hang out their tongues, 100
Lord, thou hast been our dwelling place in all generations, 23

Man is nothing but the soil of a small country, 76
My child is very sad, 134

My daughter, not all is vanity, 109

My heart is in the East, and I in the uttermost West, 61

My lord, take this delicacy in your hand, 58

My quiet prison guards, much tried. My lovers, 122

Night of sleeplessness, 105

O Lord, save we beseech Thee, 66

O that thou wert as my brother, 40

Of life and its ceasing to be, with changes of sea wind, 119

Olé. All yea. All no. No. He who is getting old and slow, 139

On the day I was born, 64

Rejoice not, O Israel, for joy, as other people, 46

Remember now thy Creator in the days of thy youth, 34

Shalom, Mount Avarim. Blessed be your slopes, 60

She turns and calls him by name, 88

Six seven minutes after death, 140

Some clouds are rainclouds, 94

Stop playing with words, you wastrels, 85

Suddenly, 145

Summer has reigned, 107

Taxis below, 132

The Almighty has dealt bitterly with me, 91

The beauty of Israel is slain upon thy high places, 17

The flowering castor, abruptly at night grown dense, 113

The hour is very weary, as before sleep, 89

The place where I have not been, 138

The rain is over, 116

The Sabbath stars have climbed high, more peaceful than you, 101

The tottering wall has underground thoughts, 120

The wind took them, light swept them all away, 73

There are many like him here, without epitaph, without a mound, 79

There is a box and a coverlet, and a pair of black horses, 92

They alone are left me; they alone still faithful, 88

Thirty-two times I went forth to my life, 128

Thus hath the Lord God shewed unto me, 49

Thus saith the Lord; for three transgressions of Moab, 48

Up rose the sun again, again the sun set, 71

War at first is like a young girl,
57
We were not like dogs among
the Gentiles . . . they pity a
dog, 98
When the Lord turned again
the captivity of Zion, 28
When they brought my father
to the mound of corpses, 95
Where are the men with the
strength to be men? 57
Where are they? where are thy
wise men? 41

With a violin in the alley grand-
father and son disappeared,
110

You have enslaved me with
your lovely body, 62
You: trapped in the homeland
of the Chosen People, 131
You walked as if in snow. And
you walked in snow, 118
Your people are drowning in
blood and you're making
poems, 80

Index of Poets

Abraham ibn Ezra, 64, 65
Alterman, Natan, 107, 108, 109, 110, 112
Amichai, Yehuda, 127, 128, 130, 131, 132, 133, 134, 136, 138
Amos, 48, 49
Avidan, David, 139, 140
Avraham Ben Yitzhak, 83, 84

Bat-Miriam, Yocheved, 102, 104
Bialik, Chaim Nachman, 71, 72, 73, 74

Carmi, T., 141, 142, 143

Ecclesiastes, 32, 34

Fichman, Yaakov, 82
Fogel, David, 89

Galai, Benjamin, 125
Gilboa, Amir, 116, 117, 118
Goldberg, Leah, 113, 114
Greenberg, Uri Zvi, 89, 90, 91, 92, 93, 94, 95, 98
Guri, Chaim, 121, 122, 124

Hillel, Omer, 145
Hosea, 46

Isaiah, 41, 43, 44

Job, 18
Judah al-Harizi, 63
Judah Halevi, 60, 61, 62, 63

Malachi, 53
Mar, Yehiel, 126
Micah, 51
Moses ibn Ezra, 59

Psalms, 20, 22, 23, 25, 27, 28, 29, 30

Rachel, 87, 88
Rokeah, David, 119, 120

Sach, Natan, 148
Samuel II, 17
Samuel the Prince, 57
Shalom, Shin, 105, 106
Shlonsky, Avraham, 99, 100, 101
Shneour, Zalman, 85
Solomon ibn Gabirol, 57, 58
Song of Solomon, The, 35, 37, 38, 40

Tchernichovsky, Saul, 76, 79, 80

Index of Translators

Adler, H. M., 66

Avidan, David, 139, 140

Everwine, Peter, 141

Friend, Robert, 71, 82, 87, 88, 105, 107, 114

Gold, Ben Zion, 89, 90, 91, 92, 93, 94

Goldstein, David, 57, 58, 60

Gutmann, Assia, 127, 131, 132, 133, 134, 136, 138

Jacobs, A. C., 73, 95

Kahn, Sholom J., 145

Lewis, Bernard, 120

Mezey, Robert, 57, 59, 60, 61, 62, 63, 64, 65, 72, 74, 76, 79, 80, 83, 84, 85, 88, 89, 90, 91, 92, 93, 94, 98, 99, 104, 106, 109, 110, 112, 116, 118, 119, 121, 125, 130, 148

Mintz, Ruth Finer, 100, 108, 117, 122, 124, 126, 128

Moraes, Dom, 89, 101, 102, 113, 142, 143

Starkman, Shula, 72, 74, 76, 79, 80, 104, 109, 110, 112, 116, 118, 119, 121, 125, 130, 141

Waxman, Meyer, 64

ABOUT THE COMPILER

The poet Robert Mezey was born and grew up in Philadelphia; he says of his childhood that it was "wretched and exalted—like everyone's." He studied at Kenyon College in Ohio and was graduated from the University of Iowa, but he feels that his education really began after he dropped out of graduate school.

Mr. Mezey's first full-length book, *The Lovemaker*, won the Lamont Poetry Award in 1960, and he is the author of several other volumes of poetry, the most recent being his selected poems, *The Door Standing Open*. He is also the co-editor of *Naked Poetry*, a widely used anthology of contemporary American verse, and the poetry editor of the magazine *TransPacific*. He has taught at several universities, but for the last five years has devoted all his time to writing and translating. With his wife and three children, he lives in Spain.

ABOUT THE ILLUSTRATOR

Moishe Smith's prints have been the subject of one-man shows in galleries and universities throughout this country and in Italy and Switzerland. His work is represented in the permanent collections of more than seventy-five museums and public collections in this country, including the Metropolitan Museum of Art, the Chicago Art Institute, the Fogg Collection of Harvard University, and in museums in West Germany, Italy, Holland, Pakistan, the Philippines and Canada.

Born in Chicago but raised in Detroit, Moishe Smith received a B.A. degree from the New School for Social Research in New York City and graduate degrees from the University of Iowa. A recipient of both a Fulbright grant and a Guggenheim fellowship, Mr. Smith has taught at Southern Illinois University and Stout State University. Recently he has been a visiting artist at the University of Wisconsin, Utah State University, and the University of Iowa.

He and his wife make their home in Italy, where he raises grapes and drinks wine.

45. 86, 4 top players (with words)
88, My dear
172, Jesus walking on the waters